Teaching About Disabilities Through Children's Literature

Recent Titles in
Through Children's Literature Series

Promoting a Global Community Through Multicultural Children's Literature
  Stanley F. Steiner

Investigating Natural Disasters Through Children's Literature: An Integrated Approach
  Anthony Fredericks

Math Links: Teaching the NCTM 2000 Standards Through Children's Literature
  Caroline W. Evans, Anne J. Leija and Trina R. Falkner

Hobbies Through Children's Books and Activities
  Nancy Allen Jurenka

The World of Work Through Children's Literature: An Integrated Approach
  Carol M. Butzow and John W. Butzow

Integrating Art and Language Arts Through Children's Literature
  Debi Englebaugh

Teaching Problem Solving Through Children's Literature
  James W. Forgan

Technology Through Children's Literature
  Holly Doe

Multicultural American History Through Children's Literature
  Kay A. Chick and Deborah Ann Ellermeyer

Character Builders: Books and Activities for Character Education
  Liz Knowles, EdD and Martha Smith

The Natural World Through Children's Literature: An Integrated Approach
  Carol M. Butzow and John W. Butzow

Much More Social Studies Through Children's Literature: A Collaborative Approach
  Anthony D. Fredericks

Teaching About Disabilities Through Children's Literature

Mary Anne Prater and Tina Taylor Dyches

A Member of the Greenwood Publishing Group

Westport, Connecticut • London

Library of Congress Cataloging-in-Publication Data

Prater, Mary Anne.
   Teaching about disabilities through children's literature / Mary Ann Prater and Tina Taylor Dyches.
     p. cm. — (Through children's literature)
   Includes bibliographical references and index.
   ISBN 978-1-59158-541-1 (alk. paper)
   1. Children's literature—History and criticism. 2. Children with disabilities in literature. I. Dyches,
Tina Taylor. II. Title.
   PN1009.5.C44P73 2008
   809'.933527—dc22   2007034917

British Library Cataloguing in Publication Data is available.

Library of Congress Catalog Card Number: 2007034917
ISBN: 978-1-59158-541-1

First published in 2008

Libraries Unlimited/Teacher Ideas Press, 88 Post Road West, Westport, CT 06881
A Member of the Greenwood Publishing Group, Inc.
www.lu.com

Printed in the United States of America

♾™

The paper used in this book complies with the
Permanent Paper Standard issued by the National
Information Standards Organization (Z39.48–1984).

10 9 8 7 6 5 4 3 2 1

Contents

I. Introduction ix
  Elements of Quality Literature ix
    Incorporation of Disabilities x
    Representation of Disabilities x
    Illustrations xi
  Portrayal of Disabilities xii
  Using Children's Books to Teach About Disabilities xiii
    Awareness xiii
    Knowledge xiii
    Understanding xiii
    Acceptance xiii
  Content of This Book xiv
  References xiv

II. Annotated Bibliography 1
  Attention-Deficit/Hyperactivity Disorder (ADD/ADHD) 2
  Autism 6
  Communication Disorders 12
  Deafness and Hard of Hearing 19
  Emotional and Behavioral Disorders 22
  Intellectual Disability 27
  Learning Disabilities 34
  Orthopedic Impairment 41
  Traumatic Brain Injury 48
  Visual Impairment and Blindness 48

III. Lesson Plans 55
  Lesson Plan 1 56
  Lesson Plan 2 57
  Lesson Plan 3 58
    Our Five Senses 59
    Ian's Walk 59
  Lesson Plan 4 61
  Lesson Plan 5 62
    Recognizing Feelings 63
    Thank You, Mr. Falker 63

IV. Unit Plans 65

The Bus People: Unit 1, Lesson 1 66
   The Stigma of Disability 66
   Trick or Treat? Activity 67
The Bus People: Unit 1, Lesson 2 68
   Intellectual Disabilities: From *Slow* to *Go!* 68
      Life Skills Activity 69
The Bus People: Unit 1, Lesson 3 70
   Communication Disorders: The Silent Ones 70
      "The Silent Ones" Script 71
The Bus People: Unit 1, Lesson 4 72
   Impact of Disabilities on Families 72
Freak the Mighty: Unit 2, Lesson 1 73
   Dispelling Stereotypes: The Unvanquished Truth 73
      Attitudes Toward Individuals with Disabilities 74
Freak the Mighty: Unit 2, Lesson 2 75
   To the Max: Success in the Face of Learning Disabilities 75
Freak the Mighty: Unit 2, Lesson 3 76
   Little Big Man: The Mighty Freak 76
      Kevin's Strengths Worksheet 77
Freak the Mighty: Unit 2, Lesson 4 78
   Real Life Heroes: Our Peers with Disabilities 78
I Am an Artichoke: Unit 3, Lesson 1 79
   Defining Normal and Abnormal Behavior 79
      What Is Normal? Part 1 80
      What Is Normal? Part 2 81
I Am an Artichoke: Unit 3, Lesson 2 82
   Understanding Persons with EBDs 82
      Emotional/Behavioral Disorders Quiz 83
      Emotional/Behavioral Disorder Quiz Answer Key 84
I Am an Artichoke: Unit 3, Lesson 3 85
   Understanding Eating Disorders 85
I Am an Artichoke: Unit 3, Lesson 4 86
   Developing Friendships: What Should I Say? 86
      Talking with Individuals with EBDs 87
Joey Pigza Loses Control: Unit 4, Lesson 1 88
   Characteristics of ADHD 88
   Simulation Activities 89
      Activity 1—Following Directions 89
      Activity 2—Paying Attention 89
      Quick Facts About ADHD 90
Joey Pigza Loses Control: Unit 4, Lesson 2 91
   Attitudes Toward Disabilities 91
      Attitudes Worksheet 92
Joey Pigza Loses Control: Unit 4, Lesson 3 93
   Treatment of ADHD 93
      ADHD Treatment Quiz 94
      ADHD Treatment Quiz Answer Key 95

Joey Pigza Loses Control: Unit 4, Lesson 4 96

    Read All About It!... 96

Tru Confessions: Unit 5, Lesson 1... 97

    Etiology of Disabilities: The Mutant Shark Person 97

        Causes of Disabilities... 98

Tru Confessions: Unit 5, Lesson 2... 99

    Avoiding Victimization: "I Don't Want to Be Different"............................ 99

        Protector, Not Perpetrator 100

Tru Confessions: Unit 5, Lesson 3.. 101

    Accepting Differences: Just Who Has Special Needs?............................. 101

        Learning Preferences Checklist 102

        Eddie's Strengths and Challenges 103

        My Strengths and Challenges 104

Tru Confessions: Unit 5, Lesson 4.. 105

    Growing Up: Spinning into Separate Futures................................... 105

        Future Planning Chart... 106

        Eddie's Future Planning Chart.. 107

V. Activities and Reproducible Worksheets 109

    Same and Different #1 110

    Same and Different #2 112

    Sibling's Reaction 114

    Feelings 115

    Write an Author 116

    Reflection Journal 117

    Attitudes... 118

    Roller-Movie 120

    Retelling in a Different Time Period 121

    Mock Children's Literature Award 122

    Book Review 123

    Write a Letter to a Character with Disabilities................................... 124

VI. Additional Resources.. 125

Attention-Deficit/Hyperactivity Disorder 125

Developmental Disabilities (Including Autism, Developmental Delay,

    Intellectual Disabilities, and Multiple Disabilities) 125

Deafness/Hard of Hearing 125

Learning Disabilities... 125

Various Disabilities.... 125

    Title Index... 127

    Author Index 129

    Award-Winning Books 131

I. Introduction

Before reading further, take thirty seconds to list all of the books or stories you can think of that include characters with disabilities.

_____   _____

_____   _____

_____   _____

_____   _____

_____   _____

Did you think of any classical literature, such as the Grimm folktales that include dwarfs, giants, and deformed witches? What about Tiny Tim in *A Christmas Carol,* Captain Ahab in *Moby Dick,* or Quasimodo in *The Hunchback of Notre Dame*? Did Pinocchio or Captain Hook come to mind? All of these are examples of characters with physical disabilities. You may have thought of characters with cognitive disabilities, such as Forrest Gump, Charly in *Flowers for Algernon*, or Lennie in *Of Mice and Men*.

What about books written primarily for children? Did your list include characters from children's literature? You might have listed Charlie, a boy in the Newbery Award–Winning *Summer of the Swans*, who has mental retardation, or Mary, Laura's older sister in the Little House on the Prairie series, who becomes blind. What about Klara in *Heidi* or Colin in *The Secret Garden*? Both Klara and Colin experience physical disabilities requiring the use of a wheelchair. Klara's disability, however, is "real," whereas Colin's is not. All four of these books are considered classics.

Many other picture and chapter books portray characters with disabilities, and these books can be used to teach children about disabilities. We wrote this book to help teachers, social workers, psychologists, counselors, parents, and librarians use children's literature effectively to help children learn about disabilities. Our book includes an annotated bibliography of more than one hundred fictional and biographical books, in addition to five lesson plan examples, five unit plan examples, reproducible worksheets, activity materials, and an index for locating books and authors. Although we've provided several tools for readers to use, we believe that those implementing these plans and activities should understand elements of quality literature, particularly in selecting books characterizing disabilities. It is at this point that we begin.

Elements of Quality Literature

Historically, many authors have used physical disabilities metaphorically to represent a character's inner traits, both positive and negative. In their folktales, the Grimm brothers portrayed witches with physical deformities and poor eyesight to represent evil. *Pinocchio*'s nose grew as his integrity diminished. On the other side of the spectrum, "crippled" Tiny Tim in *A Christmas Carol* represented kindness and love. Although all of these older stories may be found in today's classrooms, libraries, and homes, current authors and teachers consider using physical attributes to represent inner qualities to be unacceptable: stereotypical and politically incorrect. Today authors are more likely to include a character with a disability to teach about the disability, to promote sensitivity for those who are different, or simply to represent true conditions in the world in which we live.

Incorporation of Disabilities

Generally speaking, disabilities are physical or mental impairments that restrict an individual in some way. In education we generally use the disabling conditions outlined by U.S. federal legislation: the Individuals with Disabilities Education Act (IDEA). The major categories of disabilities under this Act include learning disabilities, communication disorders (speech/language impairments), mental retardation, emotional and behavior disorders, hearing impairments (including deafness), visual impairments (including blindness), autism, traumatic brain injury, and orthopedic impairments, among others. Although attention-deficit disorder is not identified as a separate category under IDEA, we have included it in this book because of its prevalence among children and adolescents.

Characters with orthopedic and sensory impairments are the most frequently portrayed in children's literature, including characters who are blind, deaf, or rely on wheelchairs. In recent years, however, an increasing number of published books are including characters with other disabilities, such as autism, attention-deficit disorder, or specific learning disabilities. We hope to see a continual increase not only in the number of books published, but in accurate portrayals of best practice for helping those with disabilities, integrated within engaging stories featuring stunning illustrations.

Federal legislation in the United States requires that all students with disabilities receive a free, appropriate public education; thus today many students with disabilities are educated in general education classrooms. This inclusion necessitates an awareness and sensitivity to their needs from their general education teachers and nondisabled classmates. Books can provide a forum to discuss characteristics of people with disabilities, environmental and attitudinal barriers they might experience, and feelings they might have while dealing with these difficulties, along with many other topics.

Representation of Disabilities

Many children's literature experts agree that six elements should be considered when determining the quality of a book: theme, characterization, setting, plot, point of view, and literary style. We address each of these briefly within the context of identifying quality books that include characterizations of disabilities.

Theme. The theme of a book answers the question, "What is the main idea of the book?" or "What was the author's intent in writing this book?" Because we have focused on fiction or storybooks, we suggest that the author's intent extend beyond teaching about the disability. We prefer for characterization of the disability to unfold as part of a well-told story. If the author's intent is solely to teach about disabilities, the nonfiction genre can effectively provide this information.

Characterization. Characterization may be viewed across several dimensions, including the role and the growth of the character. Characters may play a major, supporting, or minor role within the plot. In this book, we have included only books in which the character with a disability is in a major or supporting role. The growth of the character is also an important consideration. Characters can grow and develop as a result of what occurs in the story, or they may not change at all. Authors often use the character with a disability to influence the growth or development of a character without any disability. For example, the sister of a child with Down's syndrome may become more patient with her brother because of an event that occurred as part of the story. We believe that representing characters with disabilities only as they affect characters without disabilities does not represent the full range of contributions that individuals with disabilities make to our society.

Setting. The setting—the time and place for the story—is critical in examining books that include characters with disabilities. An accurate portrayal of the conditions for individuals with disabilities in the early 1800s, for example, is very different from portrayals in contemporary settings. Historically, individuals with disabilities were often segregated in hospitals or institutions, merely housed and cared for at individual or private expense. Today those with disabilities lead more integrated lives, with involvement in all aspects of society. When reading historical depictions of people with disabilities, children need to be educated that past practice (e.g., institutionalization) is not best practice today.

Plot. In most cases, books that portray a character with a disability use the disability as part of the plot or storyline. The role of the disability, however, may be major or minor. In some books, for example, the plot centers on the character's disability being identified and treated through special education services. Other books call attention to the disability only as necessary to the plot or the development of other characters. Regardless of the role of the disability in the storyline, characters with disabilities should be portrayed as being more alike than different from those without disabilities, emphasizing the disability only to the degree necessary to demonstrate that some differences between characters do exist.

Point of view. The point of view is the perspective from which the story is told. Often the perspective is that of a child or adolescent with a disability, particularly when the disability is not mental retardation. Studies show that mental retardation is portrayed from the point of view of the affected character in fewer books than are learning disabilities or autism (Dyches, Prater, & Cramer, 2001; Prater, 1999, 2003). When stories are told from the point of view of individuals with disabilities, readers can gain greater insight into these individuals' lives. If the story is not told from the point of view of the character with a disability, it is usually told from the perspective of a sibling or a peer. These perspectives can provide the reader insight into what it might be like to be a sibling or a friend to someone with a disability.

Literary style. The author's literary style is clarified by answering the question, "How is the story written?" The choice of words, structure of sentences, figures of speech, and so forth are elements of style that the author uses to develop the plot, characters, and setting. The literary style should be appropriate for the age level for which the story is written. The matter of appropriateness can become more complex for books written about disabilities for children with disabilities. Students with poor reading skills or cognitive abilities below age level (or both) are unable to read or enjoy books written at more complex levels. Thus ability levels as well as age of intended audience must be considered when evaluating the literary style of individual books.

Illustrations

Books written for children can be categorized as picture or chapter books. Picture books, generally targeted for young readers or nonreaders, tell a story through illustration either alone or combined with fairly simple text. Chapter books may include some illustrations, but the pictures are not essential to complete the story. Quality illustrations, including photographs, should be evaluated in terms of story interpretation and style, text enhancement, artistic quality, layout, and design.

Story interpretation and style. Quality illustrations interpret the story well. The reader should be able to "tell" the story by viewing the pictures. The style of illustrations (e.g., expressionistic, impressionistic, folk, cartoon) should be appropriate to the story and to the age level of the targeted audience. Regardless of the style, characters with disabilities should be portrayed with the physical attributes appropriate to the disability without exaggeration or distortion. If the individual with a disability has a prosthesis, such as a mechanical arm, or if the character uses a mobility device, such as a wheelchair or walker, these should also be portrayed accurately for the time period in which the story takes place.

Text enhancement. The illustrations should be consistent with the text and enhance the plot, theme, setting, and literary style of the story. Sometimes the illustrations can add information not contained in the text. For example, pictures in a book about presidents of the United States could show Franklin D. Roosevelt in a wheelchair even if the text did not mention his disability.

Art quality. The quality of the art refers to the rhythm, balance, variety, emphasis, spatial order, and unity of the illustrations. The artist may use oil, watercolor, acrylics, chalk, crayon, woodcuts, charcoal, photography, or other art media either solely or in combination. Quality art takes the viewer to a deeper and broader level of understanding than text alone.

Layout and design. The overall layout and design of the illustrations and text should be visually appealing. This includes not only each page of the story, but the cover and the leaf pages. The print size and color and the placement of the text should complement the illustrations and be easy to read.

Portrayal of Disabilities

The manner in which society perceives individuals with disabilities contributes to ways in which they are portrayed in books. Societies that perceive people with disabilities as a menace will portray them as isolated, segregated, or even punished. A society that pities them will show them as recipients of charity. If individuals with disabilities are viewed as sickly, books will show them requiring therapy or treatment. If they are perceived as more like than unlike those without disabilities, they will be shown in integrated settings having reciprocal relationships with other characters.

Fortunately, during the past thirty years, society has begun to modify beliefs about those with disabilities. These changed beliefs may be described across two areas: terminology and inclusion. Phrases such as "blind as a bat" or "deaf as a doornail" are viewed today as demeaning and inappropriate. Terms that formerly referred to specific conditions but have since taken on broader and more derogatory meaning (e.g., *imbecile, idiot*) are no longer used in the field of disabilities. Current proper terminology requires use of "person-first" language: the person comes before the disability. Thus rather than referring to "the disabled person," it is proper to say "the person who has a disability." The use of person-first language helps us remember that all individuals are unique and that a person is not defined by an ability or a disability.

The second societal change is movement toward inclusion of those with disabilities. As mentioned earlier, students with disabilities cannot be denied access to public education regardless of the severity of a disability. The trend is to provide special education services within the general education schools and classrooms. In addition, young and older adults with disabilities are more frequently employed in the community and encouraged to participate in community-sponsored events. This has not always been the case. Historically those with disabilities were segregated into hospitals and institutions and denied services available to other citizens.

Contemporary portrayals of disabilities should recognize society's current beliefs about individuals with disabilities.

- **Individuals with disabilities should be portrayed as more similar than dissimilar to individuals without disabilities.** The character should not be defined by his or her disability, but portrayed as an individual with the same human traits as others. The disability is merely one characteristic. For example, characters with disabilities should be portrayed as having thoughts, feelings, interests, and relationships that are unique to the character regardless of the disability.

- **Nondiscriminatory language (such as person-first language) should be used.** If an author has a bully use derogatory language in teasing a character with a disability, it must be balanced with positive language elsewhere in the story.

- **Characters with disabilities should appear in settings with, not isolated from, their nondisabled peers.** Such settings may include schools, places of employment, leisure activities, community events, homes, and so forth.

- **Characters with disabilities should be portrayed in reciprocal relationships.** The character with the disability should not just receive care and consideration, but should contribute something to other characters in the story.

Using Children's Books to Teach About Disabilities

Books provide windows by which children can look outside of their own experiences and live vicariously through others. Books may also be mirrors, allowing readers to look thoughtfully at themselves. When books act as both windows and mirrors, they allow children to stretch themselves beyond their circle of experience, yet reflect on similarities between themselves and characters in the book. In this way, they can learn to accept people who on the surface appear to be different.

Children's literature can promote introspection regarding awareness, knowledge, understanding, and acceptance of self and others. We discuss each of these briefly in the context of disabilities.

Awareness

Children learn through experience that humans differ by characteristics such as age, gender, size, and hair color. Yet many children's experiences with diverse groups, especially those with disabilities, are limited. Literature can expose readers to and thus raise levels of awareness of people with various disabilities. Literature can also foster awareness of basic and complex social issues such as inclusion, friendship, causation and prevention of disabilities, historical treatment of disabilities, and so forth.

Knowledge

Through literature children can learn about characteristics of those with disabilities and at the same time discover that individuals with disabilities have unique physical and personality traits, like all human beings. Children can also gain knowledge of the social issues impacting those with disabilities, historically and currently.

Understanding

After reading a quality book, readers should better understand themselves, other people, and social issues. Understanding involves a deeper level of intellectual and personal involvement than awareness or knowledge. Reading about an individual with a disability can help children understand their own feelings and reactions to those with differences. Portrayals of outdated negative attitudes and of social injustices toward those with disabilities can generate rich discussions in which readers can ask, "What would I do if I were in that situation?" or "How would I act if I had a brother with a disability?"

Acceptance

The next level, acceptance of self and others, requires emotional involvement. People can be aware of and understand human diversity but never fully accept individuals different from themselves. A powerful book may provide the impetus for change as readers come to understand on a deeper level their feelings and reactions toward those who are different. They may be shocked to see themselves in a character who torments or ignores a person with a disability, or they may see for the first time the perspective, needs, and feelings of a person like those they have marginalized in the past.

Content of This Book

In Section 1 we have introduced important concepts to consider when selecting and using children's literature portraying characters with disabilities. The remainder of the book, comprising five additional sections, focuses on using fictional children's books that can be used to teach about individuals with disabilities. Section 2 provides an annotated bibliography of books we recommend based on the criteria introduced in Section 1. We have included several Newbery Medal and Honor books that, although they may not meet all of the criteria, are widely available and often promoted by teachers and librarians and read by students. Each annotation includes the title, author, publisher, year published, interest level, plot summary, type of disability portrayed, and discussion questions. Section 3 includes five detailed lesson plans, each portraying a different disability. Each lesson plan demonstrates how teachers and others can use the books listed in the annotated bibliography to teach about disabilities at the awareness, knowledge, understanding, or acceptance level. Each lesson plan is designed to be taught in one day. Section 4 includes five unit plans. Similar to the lesson plans, the unit plans demonstrate how books can be used to teach about disabilities and other content. The unit plans, which include several lesson plans centered on the same book, can be implemented in one week. Section 5 presents reproducible worksheets and other materials for activities that tie directly to using children's literature to teach about disabilities. An index of all books and authors included in this book appears in Section 6.

"Books are the quietest and most constant of friends; they are the most accessible and wisest of counselors, and the most patient of teachers" (Eliot, 1905, p. 20). We hope you find our book to be a helpful tool as you prepare to use children's literature to teach about disabilities. We wish you happy reading and joyful teaching.

References

Dyches, T. T., Prater, M. A., & Cramer, S. (2001). Mental retardation and autism in children's books. *Education and Training in Mental Retardation and Developmental Disabilities, 36,* 230–243.

Eliot, C. W. (1905). *The happy life.* New York: Crowell.

Prater, M. A. (1999). Characterization of mental retardation in children and young adult literature. *Education and Training in Mental Retardation and Developmental Disabilities, 34,* 418–431.

Prater, M. A. (2003). Learning disabilities in children's and adolescent literature: How are characters portrayed? *Learning Disability Quarterly, 26,* 47–62.

II. Annotated Bibliography

In this annotated bibliography each book is listed under the category of the disability portrayed. Within the boxed section you will find:

> 📖 **Title**, Author, (illustrator, if appropriate), year published, readability/interest level, awards (if granted).
>
> Each boxed section is followed by a plot summary and discussion questions. The discussion questions for chapter books are listed by chapter. The books are alphabetized by book title under the alphabetized category of disability. The index in the back lists all books by title and author.

Attention-Deficit/Hyperactivity Disorder (ADD/ADHD)

A.D.D. not B.A.D. by Audrey Penn (Monica Dunsky Wyrick). 2003. Grade K+
Eight-year-old Josh hates being unable to concentrate or control himself, but with the help of his parents, his teacher, and a doctor, he learns to deal with his condition, known as ADHD (attention-deficit/hyperactivity disorder).

- Why did Mr. Jugardor have the kids in his class walk around in each other's shoes?

- How did Mr. Jugardor help the class understand how Jimmy felt?

- How would you act with a ladybug down your back?

- What do you think would be hard for Jimmy because he has ADHD?

The ADDed Touch by Robyn Watson (Susanne Nuccio). 2000. Grade K+
Matthew, a first grader, has trouble staying focused, following directions, and controlling himself, until he is diagnosed with ADD.

- What are some of the words that rhyme in this story?

- What are some of the things that are hard for Matthew to do? Are they hard for you?

- What does the doctor tell Matthew and his mother?

- Do all children who don't pay attention have ADD?

Eddie Enough! by Debbie Zimmett (Charlotte Murray Fremaux). 2001. Grade 2+
Eddie Minetti doesn't mind being called Eddie Spaghetti until it gets changed to Eddie Enough. On a very bad day at school, Eddie can't seem to do anything right. His teacher tells him she's had "enough, Eddie, enough" and his classmates rename him. Eddie is soon diagnosed and prescribed medicine. Eddie learns how to become Eddie Just Right.

- Why did Eddie like his nickname Eddie Spaghetti, but not his nickname Eddie Enough?

- Do you or anyone you know have a nickname? Do you like it? Why or why not?

- What were some of the things that happened on the worst day of Eddie's life?

- Why did Eddie meet with a doctor? What did they do?

- Do you know anyone with ADHD? If so, how are they the same or different from Eddie?

- What does S.T.A.R. mean? How could you use S.T.A.R.?

I'm Somebody Too by Jeanne Gehret. 1992. Grade 4+

Emily feels left out and alone when her parents devote so much time to her younger brother, Ben, who has ADD. After his disorder is diagnosed, she has conflicting feelings as he is praised for doing things she has always done.

Chapters 1–3: Have you ever felt alone like Emily does? When and where?

Chapters 4–6: Why do you think Ben's condition is to be kept a secret?

Chapters 7–9: Why do you think Ben's mother expects his teacher to do something different for him during the spelling test? What could she have done?

Chapters 10–12: What does Emily learn about ADD from Dr. Bernstein?

Chapters 13–14: Does Emily have reason to be resentful of Ben? Have you ever felt that way? When and where?

Chapters 15–18: How has Ben changed or not changed since the beginning of the story?

Chapters 19–22: Why is Emily having difficulty accepting the changes in Ben?

Chapters 23–25: What does Emily mean by saying Ben was taking two steps backward? What does this say about treating ADD?

Joey Pigza Loses Control by Jack Gantos. 2000. Grade 4+ (Joey Pigza Series #2), Newbery Honor Book

Joey, who has ADHD, goes to live with his father and grandmother for the summer. His father is convinced that Joey doesn't need his medication and flushes it down the toilet. Then things begin to really get out of control.

Chapters 1–2: How has Joey's medication helped him? Do you think Joey will be happy staying with his father and grandmother? Why or why not?

Chapters 3–4: How are Joey and his father alike? How are they different?

Chapters 5–6: Joey feels like two different people at the same time. What does that mean? Have you ever felt like that? Why and when?

Chapters 7–8: What does batting remind Joey about? Why didn't Joey's dad want Joey to wear his patch? Do you think he's right or wrong? Why?

Chapters 9–10: What does the word "normal" mean to you? Do you think Joey is normal? Why or why not?

Chapters 11–12: How is Joey acting differently since he stopped taking his medicine? When does Joey finally realize it was a mistake not to take his medicine?

Chapters 13–14: Why is Joey not at all like his father? Will he see his father again? Why or why not?

Joey Pigza Swallowed the Key by Jack Gantos. 1998. Grade 4+ (Joey Pigza Series #1)

Joey has a hard time paying attention, sitting still, and thinking before he acts. He is always getting in trouble at school for being out of control. Joey and his mom, along with some professionals, try to get Joey the help he needs to be able to function in school.

Chapters 1–2: What does it mean to be "wired"? What do you think really happened to Joey's grandma?

Chapters 3–4: What kinds of things does Joey do with the doctor at the clinic? Why is Joey afraid to go to the special education class? Should he be? How might the special class help him?

Chapters 5–6: Describe a good and a bad day for Joey. Describe a good and bad day for you.

Chapters 7–8: What does the word "special" mean to you? Why do you think so many bad things happen to Joey?

Chapters 9–10: Which present do you think Joey likes the best? Why? What are some of the bad decisions Joey has made?

Chapters 11–12: Dr. Preston tells Joey that he will be OK. Do you agree? Why or why not? Why does Joey really want a dog?

Chapters 13–15: How is Joey's new medicine different from his old medicine? What does Joey mean by, "I felt like Christmas was just a few days away even though it wasn't"?

Pay Attention, Slosh! by Mark Smith. 1997. Grade 2+

Eight-year-old Josh has trouble concentrating and controlling his behavior, and he hates being called Slosh. But with the help of his parents, teacher, and doctor, he learns to live with ADHD.

Chapters 1–2: Why do you think it's so hard for Josh to pay attention and sit still? Do you ever have these problems? When?

Chapters 3–4: What distracts Josh? Why do you think he always get in trouble?

Chapters 5–6: Why does Josh visit Dr. Hartnett? What does she tell him?

Chapters 7–8: How do Josh's parents and his teacher help him change?

Chapters 9–10: What does Dr. Harnett suggest for Josh? Did it help? If so, in what ways? Would they help you? Why or why not?

Phoebe's Best Best Friend by Barbara Roberts. 2000. Grade 4+ (Phoebe Flower's Adventures #3)

Even though third grader Phoebe is having trouble concentrating on her school work, through her writing she discovers the true meaning of "best friend."

Chapters 1–2: Why is Phoebe so excited to have a best friend? Do you have a best friend? Do you feel the same way about your best friend?

Chapters 3–4: Do you think Gloria is really Phoebe's best friend? Why or why not?

Chapters 5–6: Do you think Phoebe had the best or the worst day ever? Why? What was your best and worst day ever?

Chapters 7–8: What was Phoebe's mom's secret? How do you think Phoebe felt when she heard her mom's secret?

Chapter 9: How does Phoebe's thinking in a different way make her a heroine but also get her in trouble? Has that ever happened to you?

Waiting for Mr. Goose by Laurie Lears (Karen Ritz). 1999. Grade K+

Stephen, a boy with ADHD, overcomes his difficulty sitting still to free a wild goose that limps because of a steel trap on its leg.

• What is hard about life for Stephen? How do his problems make him feel?

• Why does Stephen want to be like the geese he watches?

• How is Stephen able to make himself be patient?

• How does learning to wait help Stephen?

• How can we learn when to wait, and when to be like the geese?

Zipper, the Kid with ADHD by Caroline Janover. 1997. Grade 4+

Zipper, whose real name is Zach, is impulsive, and he has difficulty paying attention. He always gets in trouble at home and school until he meets a retired jazz musician who tells him he would be a great drummer.

Chapters 1–3: What are Zach's strengths and limitations? Which do you think are the most important? What are your strengths and limitations?

Chapters 4–6: How well does Zach do in social situations? What does Mrs. Ginsberg teach him about making and keeping friends? What have you learned about friends?

Chapters 7–9: Do you think Zach will earn the $35 he needs for a drum set? Why or why not?

Chapters 10–12: What does Josh teach Zach about being organized? Does it appear to be helping him? Would it help you? Why or why not?

Chapters 13–15: Why do you think Zach can concentrate well while playing Nintendo or baseball but has problems paying attention in other situations? Are you like that? If so, in what situations?

Chapters 16–18: On the basis of what you've learned about Zach and Josh, what are some similarities and differences between dyslexia and ADHD?

Chapters 19–21: What do Zach and his parents think Ritalin will do for him? Do you think they are right?

Chapters 22–23: Does the ending surprise you? Why or why not? Do you think Zach will achieve his goals? Why or why not?

Autism

Adam's Alternative Sports Day by Jude Welton. 2005. Grade 4+

Nine-year-old Adam, who has Asperger syndrome, participates in an Alternative Sports Day in which he competes with intellectual rather than physical activities. Winning the Challenge Cup is very important to Adam, and with the help of an astute teacher and a good friend, Josie, Adam accepts the outcome of the competition. This story has alternative endings, demonstrating the "element of chance in everyone's life."

Chapters 1–3: What are Adam's special interests?

Chapters 4–5: How does Adam feel toward James after the first challenge?

Chapters 6–7: Why does Adam look forward to the math competition?

Chapters 8–9: What is Adam's response to Josie's winning first place in the math quiz?

Chapters 10–11: How does group work help Adam's team win?

Chapter 12: Whose act of bravery does Josie describe in her story?

Chapters 13A and 14A: What does Adam learn from the first ending when he loses the Challenge Cup?

Chapters 13B and 14B: How does Adam feel in the second ending when he wins the Challenge Cup?

Summary: How does the moral from Aesop's fable "The Tortoise and the Hare" relate to Adam's achievements and losses in the story?

Al Capone Does My Shirts by Gennifer Choldenko. 2004. Grade 5+, Newbery Honor Book

In 1935, twelve-year-old Moose Flanagan and his family move to Alcatraz so that his father can work as a prison guard, and Natalie, Moose's fifteen-year-old sister who has a disability recognized today as autism, can go to a special school. However, Natalie is denied admission to the school until Moose and the prison warden's daughter get help from the most notorious criminal on the island, Al Capone.

Chapters 1–4: How does Moose deal with Natalie's inconsistency in how she responds to him? Sometimes she ignores Moose, other times she repeats what he says, sometimes she is "tricked" into doing what he wants her to do, and, rarely, she looks him in the eye.

Chapters 5–10: What does Mrs. McCraw mean when she says, "No use throwing good after bad"? Do you agree with Mrs. McCraw? Why or why not?

Chapter 11: What kind of treatments do Natalie's parents investigate to help her get better? How do these treatments differ from those used for children with autism today?

Chapters 12–13: What does Mrs. Flanagan mean when she says, "If Natalie's going to change, we have to change first?" Why do you think Moose is given most of the responsibility to watch after Natalie?

Chapters 14–17: How would you describe "Natalie-World"? What would you like about living in this type of a world?

Chapters 18–24: How is Natalie part of the group of friends? Why do you think Moose begins to enjoy spending time with her?

Chapters 25–27: How does Moose feel about leaving Natalie alone while he searches for a baseball? Why is he afraid of the man sitting beside Natalie?

Chapters 28–32: Moose gets mad at Natalie for throwing a tantrum and claims, "I think you don't even try and I hate you for it, Natalie. We try so hard and you don't" (p. 168). Do you think he is right? How is Moose trying to help Natalie? How are his parents trying to help?

Chapter 33: When Onion holds Natalie's hand, Moose says, "This is terrible. This is good" (p. 185). What do you think he means by these contradictory statements?

Chapters 34–40: How did Natalie get admitted to the school? Do you think Moose's letter to Al Capone had anything to do with it? How do you think life will be different for Moose and his family if Natalie goes away to school?

A Corner of the Universe by Ann M. Martin. 2002. Grade 5+, Newbery Honor Book
During the summer of 1960, Hattie turns twelve years old, and her previously predictable small-town life changes drastically when her twenty-one-year-old uncle, Adam, who has many characteristics of autism, comes home from the institution. Hattie takes immediately to Adam, even when the rest of the family has trouble dealing with him.

Chapters 1–3: How do you think Hattie feels about Adam?

Chapters 4–5: How did Hattie's parents describe Adam's disabilities? How would you describe his "problems" using modern terminology? Why do you think Hattie had not heard the words "schizophrenic" or "autistic?"

Chapters 6–8: What do you think Adam meant when he told Hattie that she could "lift the corners of our universe?"

Chapters 9–12: How do Hattie's expectations of Adam compare with Nana's expectations?

Chapters 13–15: How are both Adam and Hattie "aliens?"

Chapters 16–17: Adam is thrilled at being in "the center of the universe" until the ferris wheel gets stuck. How is Adam's reaction extreme?

Chapters 18–19: Do people with disabilities have the right to have relationships with the opposite sex? Why or why not? Why do you think Adam went to extreme measures when he felt rejected by Angel?

Chapters 20–21: How is Adam rejected and ignored by his family? How does Hattie accept him?

Chapter 22: How does Adam "lift the corners of our universe?" How do other characters lift the corners of their universe?

The Curious Incident of the Dog in the Night-Time by Marc Haddon. 2003. Grades 9+, Dolly Gray Award

Christopher John Francis Boone is a fifteen-year-old boy with autism who finds his neighbor's dog, Wellington, dead on the front lawn. Christopher is arrested for killing the dog but is released and goes to great lengths to solve the mystery of who actually committed the act. *Caution: This book contains strong language.*

Chapters 2–5: Did you notice that the book begins with Chapter 2 rather than Chapter 1? Why do you think the author did this?

Chapters 7–29: Christopher is fascinated with numbers but has difficulty reading people's emotions. How do his strengths compensate for his weaknesses?

Chapters 31–53: How are similes and metaphors confusing to Christopher? Why do you think Christopher believes that similes are not lies unless they are bad ones?

Chapters 59–67: Christopher is a literal thinker. For example, he mentions that people break rules all the time, while walking across the grass or speeding, or when Christians kill in spite of the injunction, "Thou shalt not kill." How does his literal thinking help Christopher? How does it hinder him?

Chapters 71–83: How does Christopher distinguish between being "stupid," having "special needs," or having "learning difficulties"? How does Christopher think of himself?

Chapters 89–107: Why does Christopher like the subject of math? How does his interest in math relate to his interest in Sherlock Holmes?

Chapters 109–149: How does Christopher's relationship with his father differ from his relationship with Siobhan?

Chapters 151–181: Describe some examples of how Christopher has difficulty understanding the minds or intentions of others.

Chapters 191–223: How does Christopher's way of viewing the world help him to find his mother? How does it complicate his journey?

Chapters 229–233: Upon returning home to Swindon, Christopher is frightened. What does Christopher do to allay his fears?

Crow Boy by Taro Yashima (Taro Yashima). 1955. Grade K+, Caldecott Honor Book

Chibi is a young boy who displays characteristics of autism. He is different from the other children and is often left alone while his classmates study and play. After five years of school, a friendly new teacher discovers that Chibi can imitate the sounds of crows and lets Chibi participate in the talent show. His classmates realize they have misjudged Chibi.

• How do you think Chibi feels when he is alone in the classroom and at playtime?

• How do Chibi's classmates treat him before his teacher notices Chibi's special talent? Why do you think they learn to accept Chibi?

• How does Chibi remain dedicated to his education even though he isn't accepted by his classmates for so many years?

Ian's Walk by Laurie Lears (Karen Ritz). 1998. Grade 1+, Dolly Gray Award

Julie and Tara take their younger brother, Ian, on a walk to the park, but Julie gets frustrated with Ian because he takes a lot of time to explore his environment in unusual ways. When Julie takes her eyes off of Ian for a brief moment, she discovers that he is missing and is unable to find him until she begins to think like he does.

- When Julie and Tara walk with Ian to the park, how does Ian see, hear, smell, feel, and taste things differently from how they do?

- How does Julie react when Ian:

  – wants to come to the park with Julie?
  – watches the fan?
  – listens to something Julie can't hear?
  – smells the brick wall?
  – puts his head down on the ground?
  – eats leftover cereal?
  – runs away?

- How would you react to Ian when he does these things?

- Why do Julie's feelings change regarding Ian's "different" behavior?

Jackson Whole Wyoming by Joan Clark. 2005. Grades 4+

Fifth-grader Tyler Carson feels different from others because he stutters. When he is chosen to give a farewell present to his classmate, Jackson Thomas, he is reluctant to be grouped with other "weirdos." However, Tyler learns that although Jackson has Asperger syndrome, he has many strengths, interests, and abilities. Tyler learns to accept Jackson as a friend.

Chapter 1: Why is Tyler selected to give a book to Jackson? How does he react to this privilege?

Chapters 2–3: Why is Tyler unsure whether he is Jackson's friend?

Chapter 4: What does Tyler's cousin, Drew, have in common with Jackson?

Chapters 5–6: What does Jackson do when Mrs. Howard asks him to "straighten up?" What does she really want him to do?

Chapter 7–10: How does Jackson's mom's comment about looking for the good in Jackson "instead of trying to figure out the name of his problem" help Tyler understand Jackson better?

Chapters 11–12: How does Tyler feel when he learns that Jackson has Asperger syndrome? Why do you think Jackson isn't allowed to tell anyone that he has Asperger syndrome?

Chapters 13–15: Why does Tyler feel unworthy of giving the book to Jackson?

Chapters 16–17: What is the significance of "Jackson Whole Wyoming"? What does Jackson think the teacher meant?

Chapters 18–21: Why do you think Tyler calls his poem "Sometimes"?

My Brother Sammy by Becky Edwards (David Armitage). 1999. Grade K+, Dolly Gray Award

Sammy's brother expresses his feelings about having a "special" brother: he feels sad, embarrassed, lonely, and frustrated about this. After Sammy knocks down his brother's block tower, the brother gets angry. He yells that he doesn't want a special brother. But then he learns that *he* is Sammy's special brother, which helps him to see life from a new perspective.

- Why do you think Sammy's brother doesn't go to the same school as he does? Do you know kids who learn "in a different way" who go to your school? How do they get the special help they need?

- Why do you think Sammy's brother feels sad, embarrassed, lonely, and frustrated? What would you do if you were Sammy's brother?

- How is Sammy's brother a "special brother"?

- Why do you think Sammy's brother starts to enjoy doing things the way Sammy does them?

Rules by Cynthia Lord. 2006. Grade 4+, Newbery Honor Book

It seems that the more twelve-year-old Catherine tries to teach her brother David the rules of life, the more he breaks them. Worried about not being embarrassed by David's autistic behavior in public, Catherine forgets about her own. She tries to befriend a new neighbor, Kristi, and feels embarrassed that Kristi will know she is friends with Jason, who uses a communication book and a wheelchair. *Note: The chapters in this book are not numbered. For convenience, we list the questions and corresponding chapters in their numerical order.*

Chapters 1–3: Why is it important for Catherine to teach David the rules? Would you feel the same way if you had a sibling with autism? Why or why not?

Chapters 4–6: Why do you think Catherine is nervous about meeting her new neighbor?

Chapters 7–9: How does the following rule apply to the various relationships in the story: "Some people think they know who you are, when really they don't"?

Chapters 10–11: Why doesn't Catherine like Ryan Deschaine? What are some of the things he has done to Catherine and David?

Chapters 12–13: Mrs. Morehouse and Jason's speech therapist talk about him in front of him. How do you think that makes Jason feel? How would you feel if people were talking about you, but you couldn't tell them you wanted them to stop?

Chapters 14–15: How does Jason feel about Catherine? Do you think this feeling is difficult for him to express?

Chapters 16–17: Why do you think it is important to Jason that Catherine draw him in his wheelchair and not how she sees him?

Chapters 18–19: Is Catherine embarrassed by Jason, or is she embarrassed by herself? How would you respond if someone with a disability asked you to a dance?

Chapters 20–22: How does the rule "Looking closer can make something beautiful" apply to the various relationships throughout this story?

Tacos Anyone? by Marvie Ellis (Jenny Loehr). 2005. Grade K+ (An Autism Story Book #2)

Thomas doesn't understand why his four-year-old brother, Michael, behaves in unusual ways. However, when Thomas watches Michael in therapy, he learns how to interpret Michael's behavior, and they are able to play together. This book is written in both English and Spanish.

- How does Michael need "more help listening, learning, and playing"?

- What does Thomas learn about Michael when he watches him carefully?

- How can we communicate what we want or don't want without using words?

Trevor Trevor by Diane Twachtman-Cullen (Deidre Sassano). 1998. Grade 2+

Trevor is a second grader in Miss Grayley's class, where he has trouble fitting in with his classmates, who bully and tease him. His teacher designs a way to highlight Trevor's strengths, and when he helps his class win a puzzle competition, Trevor becomes the class hero. Although Trevor has autism, the disorder itself is not mentioned in the story to allow flexibility in discussing differences and similarities among children.

- Why do you think Miss Grayley is concerned about Trevor's participation in class activities?

- If you were Trevor's friend, what could you do to stop the bullies from chanting, "Trevor Trevor, not so clever"?

- What are some things Trevor can do that are difficult for his classmates to do?

- Do you think Clifford will continue to bully Trevor, or will he begin to be his friend? Why or why not?

Yolonda's Genius by Carol Fenner. 1995. Grade 4+, Newbery Honor Book

When a friend at school suggests that eleven-year-old Yolonda might be a genius, she realizes that the term "genius" more aptly describes her first-grade brother, Andrew, who struggles with reading and exhibits characteristics of autism. Yolonda is determined to convince the world of Andrew's special musical gifts, even as her family struggles to cope with the challenges of a starkly altered way of life.

Chapters 1–2: How should you act if people make fun of you for being different? What if they make fun of you for being good?

Chapters 3–4: Why does Yolonda see Andrew differently than others see him? What are some of the differences she recognizes?

Chapters 5–7: What should you do if bullies are bothering people you know?

Chapters 8–9: Why does Yolonda try to solve Andrew's problems herself? What could she do differently?

Chapters 10–12: How does Mr. Watts make a connection with Andrew? Do you think it will help his reading skills? Why or why not?

Chapters 13–14: Why do you think Momma reacted to Yolonda and Andrew's concert so negatively? What do you think makes them play such different music?

Chapters 15–16: How did Andrew make sense of the music at the blues festival? What evidence is there in this chapter that Mr. Watts's strategies are helping?

Chapter 17: What do you think Andrew means by "words that closed you in a box"?

Chapter 18: How will each member of the family's lives be different because of what happened at the blues festival? What do you predict will happen to each of them now?

Summary: How does the title *Yolonda's Genius* fit the story? In what ways do the characters in this book "rearrange old material in a way never seen before?"

Communication Disorders

Ben Has Something to Say: A Story About Stuttering by Laurie Lears (Karen Ritz). 2000. Grade K+

Ben doesn't like to talk or read aloud because he stutters. On a trip to the junkyard with his father, Ben befriends Spike, a guard dog at the junkyard that Ben wants to rescue from being sent to the pound. However, Ben must overcome his fear of speaking to ask the owner if he can buy Spike.

- Ben's stuttering keeps him from doing things he loves to do, like reading aloud in class. Have you ever been afraid to do something you love?

- Why won't Ben's father talk to Mr. Wayne for him?

- After adopting Spike, Ben is excited to tell everyone at school about his new dog. Do you think he will be able to overcome his shyness and embarrassment about his stuttering to actually tell them?

Bird Boy by Elizabeth Starr Hill. 1999. Grade 2+

Chang was born mute but can make sounds understandable to the cormorant birds his father raises to catch fish. He is teased by a boy in the village, Jinan, who calls Chang "Bird Boy." Chang garners the strength to stand up to Jinan's bullying, demonstrating his potential to become a leader despite his disability.

Chapters 1–2: How does Chang react when Jinan teases him about not being able to talk?

Chapters 3–4: Describe Chang's relationships with the birds.

Chapters 5–6: Why is Chang reluctant to be friends with Mei Mei?

Chapters 7–8: How is Chang like the little bird that never gave up?

Blabber Mouth by Morris Gleitzman. 1992. Grade 4+

Rowena ("Ro") Batts is a "blabbermouth" even though she cannot speak. When she and her dad move into a new town, she thinks his outlandish behavior will prevent her from making friends, but she learns that her friends will accept her as she is, just as she accepts her father for who he is.

Chapter 1: What does Rowena's letter to the class reveal about her disability and how she feels about it?

Chapters 2–4: How does Erin's death affect Ro's life and the way she approaches making friends?

Chapters 5–6: Ro portrays her relationship with her father as being almost perfect, yet she can't tell him how she feels about his behavior in public. Why?

Chapters 7–8: Compare and contrast what you know about Rowena and Amanda's relationships with their fathers. How does this affect their behavior and their friendship?

Chapters 9–10: Rowena can hear, even though she cannot speak. Why does her father still use sign language when he talks to her?

Chapters 11–15: Explain Mrs. Cosgrove's statement: "That poor kid's got two afflictions and I don't know which is the worst." Do you agree with her?

Chapters 16–18: Is Rowena's father really "his own worst enemy"?

Chapters 19–25: Rowena says "I'm not dumb." How does that statement have more than one meaning?

The Flimflam Man by Darleen Bailey Beard. 1998. Grade 3+

Ten-year-old Bobbie Jo is smitten with Mr. Morrison, an advance man for the traveling circus, in part because he gives her hope to overcome her stuttering.

Chapter 1: Do you think F. Bam Morrison notices Clara's stutter, or is he just ignoring it? Why?

Chapters 2–3: What does Bobbie Jo mean when she says, "I sound like a broken record"?

Chapters 4–5: Why does Bobbie Jo change her mind about her feelings for Clara Jean?

Chapters 6–9: What does Mr. Morrison mean when he says, "Some things don't work out the way you want them to. But they always work out in the end"?

Chapters 10–11: How does Bobbie Jo feel about her stuttering?

Chapters 12–13: Why do you think Mr. Morrison lies about the reel-to-reel tape recorder?

Chapter 14: Clara Jean stops teasing Bobbie Jo about her stuttering after Bobbie Jo hugged her. Why?

Epilogue: Even though Mr. Morrison takes money from the townspeople, Bobbie Jo is thankful for him. Why?

Flying Solo by Ralph Fletcher. 1998. Grade 4+

After learning of the sudden death of a classmate who was "slow" and who had a crush on her, Rachel White becomes mute. She regains confidence in her voice following a confrontation with another sixth-grade student during a day when their substitute teacher fails to show up to class. The chapters in this book are not numbered.

"Rachel White": Rachel feels that she has "the right to remain silent." Why do you think Tommy's death has such a profound impact on her?

"Kids Rule!!!": Rachel compares her feelings to a passage in her book about flying. She says she feels like a bird, "strong and hollow, filled with air and silence." What does she mean?

"Flashdrafts": How do the statements on the story list relate to some of the characters in the story?

"Music": Rachel wants to join her class in singing so much that the music made her "feel the beginnings of sound rising from some deep, buried place at the bottom of her chest." Why do you think she suppresses this feeling?

"Snack": Do you agree with Mr. Snickenberger that Rachel is trying to fly away from her problems? Why or why not?

"Connections": What similar traits do Sean and Rachel share?

"Enrichment": Why does Rachel finally allow herself to smile?

"Rock Ritual": Why does Rachel accuse Bastian of being mean to Tommy Feathers? What effect does her words have on the rest of the class?

"Tommy Feathers": What similarities and differences can you describe in the classmates' perceptions of Tommy Feathers?

"Room 238": Why do you think Fletcher chose "Flying Solo" as the title of this book?

Getting Near to Baby by Audrey Couloumbis. 1999. Grade 6+, Newbery Honor Book

Willa Jo and Little Sister have been sent to live with their aunt and uncle after the death of their younger sister, Baby. Little Sister, who hasn't spoken since the death of Baby, has difficulty adjusting to a new lifestyle and is a source of embarrassment to Aunt Patty.

Chapters 1–2: When did Little Sister lose her ability to speak? How does she communicate?

Chapters 3–6: Why does Willa Jo sometimes envy Little Sister's inability to speak? What difficulties does it cause when Little Sister is not talking?

Chapters 7–8: Why doesn't Little Sister speak, according to the doctor? What is Liz's opinion about helping Little Sister to begin talking again?

Chapters 9–10: What does Cynthia think about Little Sister? What is Willa's Jo reaction to Cynthia's ideas?

Chapters 11–14: What does Aunt Patty suggest to make Little Sister speak? How does Willa Jo react to this suggestion?

Chapters 15–16: What skills is Willa Jo able to teach Little Sister without using language?

Chapters 17–25: When does Little Sister begin speaking again? What reason does she give for not speaking?

Gold in the Hills by Laurie Lawlor. 1995. Grade 4+

After their mother's death, ten-year-old Hattie and her twelve-year-old brother Pheme are left by their father with Couzin Tirzah while he searches for gold. Pheme, who doesn't speak much because of his stuttering, becomes an object of other children's mocking. Old Judge recognizes Pheme and Hattie's talents and teaches them the meaning of forgiveness.

Chapter 1: What kind of relationship does Hattie have with her brother? How does Pheme learn about people?

Chapter 2: What do people in Cousin Tirzah's house think about Pheme? Why do they make this assumption?

Chapters 3–4: Why is Pheme's sketchbook so dear to him? What is dear to you? Why?

Chapters 5–6: Why do think Old Judge wants Pheme to speak for himself?

Chapters 7–9: What skill does Old Judge teach Pheme? What does Hattie notice about her brother for the first time after he reloads his gun?

Chapters 10–14: Why do you think Pheme stops stuttering while he was trapped under the bear?

Chapters 15–17: In your opinion, what does Pheme teach his sister and other people by his example? Who has taught you something by example?

Hooway for Wodney Wat by Helen Lester (Lynn Munsinger). 1999. Grade K+

Rodney Rat cannot say his name properly because he can't pronounce his r's. When a new student bullies Rodney's classmates, Rodney becomes the hero because of his speech problem.

• How do you think Rodney feels about not being able to pronounce his r's?

• Why doesn't Rodney just ignore the rodents when they tease him about his speech?

• Do you think everyone in the class is afraid of Camilla Capybara? Why or why not?

• When does Rodney start to feel confident?

• How do Rodney's speech problems help the other rodents accept him?

King of the Wind by Marguerite Henry. 1948. Grade 6+, Newbery Medal Book

Agba is a mute slaveboy in Morocco, Africa. He and his horse, Sham, were selected from the royal stable to be sent to France as a generous gift for King Louis XV. The boy keeps his promise to take care of Sham until the horse dies and goes through many difficulties. He risks his life many times to save his horse from suffering.

Chapters 1–5: What is Agba attached to? What do you think draws the boy and Sham closer to each other?

Chapters 6–10: How is Agba treated when he arrives in France?

Chapters 11–12: How do Agba and the horse communicate? How does the boy find Sham?

Chapters 13–14: What sounds does Agba add to his voice after he sees a cat?

Chapters 15–18: How does Agba communicate with people? How does he express his emotions?

Chapters 19–23: How does Agba let all the people in town know that Sham is the fastest racehorse? Who do you think is able to "sing," "talk," and "laugh" for Agba during moments when he desires it?

Little Women Next Door by Sheila Solomon Klass. 2000. Grade 4+

When a group of people known as the Consociates move in next door, ten-year-old Susan, who doesn't speak much because she stutters, finds a new friend in one of the new neighbors, Louisa May Alcott. Despite the unique beliefs and practices of the Consociates, Susan and her family gradually accept and come to love Louisa and her friends.

Chapter 1: In what ways does Susan's stuttering influence her daily activities? How does Aunt Nell react when Susan stutters?

Chapters 2–3: How does Louisa teach Susan to control her stuttering?

Chapters 4–6: What influence do the new neighbors have on Susan's stuttering?

Chapters 7–15: What does Pa mean when he says, "Your husband untied her tongue"? How did he "untie her tongue"?

Mary Marony and the Snake by Suzy Kline. 1991. Grade 1+

Mary Marony, a second-grade student, worries about attending a new school where she fears others will make fun of her stuttering. Although Mary makes new friends, Marvin teases her. With encouragement from her mother, who also stuttered when she was a child, Mary agrees to go to speech therapy. This is the first book in a series.

Chapter 1: Although Mary is embarrassed about her stuttering, she thinks that "maybe things wouldn't be as bad as she thought." Why?

Chapter 2: How and why does Mary break her no-fail plan for not saying any "m" words for the day?

Chapter 3: Why do you think Mary didn't stutter in the jump-rope song even though there were many "m" sounds?

Chapter 4: If she hates her stuttering so much, why doesn't Mary want to go to speech therapy to learn to overcome it?

Chapter 5: Miss Lawton tells Mary that she understands how she feels. Do you think she really does? How?

Chapter 6: When the snake escapes, Mary is the only one to remain calm. Even Mrs. Bird becomes nervous and begins to stutter a little. When the snake is found, even Marvin congratulates Mary. What is the author trying to teach us with this ending?

Ruby Mae Has Something to Say by David Small. 1992. Grade K+
Miss Ruby Mae Foote's dream is to speak at the United Nations in New York City; however, she has speech problems. With the help of her nephew, she is able to deliver her message.

- Why do people in town call Ruby Mae a "goofball"?

- What does Ruby Mae's nephew do to help deliver her message? Do you think an invention like this would really work? Why or why not?

- Do you think Ruby Mae believes Billy Bob when he says, "You don't need that old piece of junk on your head to speak well. It's all in your mind"? Why or why not?

- What is the significance of the message Ruby Mae delivers to the people at the United Nations?

The Shiniest Rock of All by Nancy Ruth Patterson. 1991. Grade 3+
Robert Reynolds is teased for the way he says his r's, but he garners courage to correct this speech impediment by going to speech therapy.

Chapters 1–3: Why do you think Robert hates the way his name is said? How could Robert have reacted differently to Ashley when she teased him?

Chapters 4–7: What do you think could be worse for Robert than not saying his r's right? Robert had the courage to see the speech therapist so people wouldn't make fun of his speech the rest of his life. Is there something you have had the courage to change in your life?

Chapters 8–10: How does Robert's dare with Chucky change the way he treats him?

Chapters 11–12: What are some of the judgments made about the following characters: Robert, Chucky, Ashley, Leslie, Mrs. Sneed? How do the perceptions of these characters change or stay the same throughout the story? Do you think Robert has confidence that his speech will improve? Why or why not?

The Silent Spillbills by Tor Seidler. 1998. Grade 4+

Katerina is a seventh grader in a new school and is self-conscious about her stuttering problem. When she becomes involved in saving a species of bird that she has named the silent spillbills, she learns to solve some of her own problems.

Chapters 1–4: How do Katerina's father and grandfather react to her stuttering about the snowball? Is her father too lenient? Is her grandfather too harsh? Which attitude might help Katerina the most?

Chapters 5–7: Whose reaction do you think Katerina was most worried about after her little speech at the party?

Chapters 8–9: Do you think Katerina would rather people feel sorry for her or make fun of her stutter? Why?

Chapters 10–11: Katerina compares herself to the silent spillbills. Is her comparison reasonable?

Chapters 12–13: What is the significance of the chapter title, "The Crow"?

Chapters 14–16: What is the "Excruciating Notion"?

Chapters 17–18: In what ways do Katerina's family support or not support her?

Chapters 19–21: Do you think Katerina and her mother are celebrating Katerina's having given her speech successfully or the possibility of having saved the spillbills?

Epilogue: What do you think it is that actually helps Katerina to start overcoming her stuttering? Do you agree with her father?

Tending to Grace by Kimberly Newton Fusco. 2004. Grade 6+

Life changes for fourteen-year-old Cornelia Thornhill when her mother runs off to Las Vegas with a boyfriend and leaves Cornelia with an eccentric aunt for an indefinite period of time. Cornelia learns to accept herself, regardless of her stuttering, and also to accept others regardless of their eccentricities and differences.

Chapters 1–5: What does Cornelia mean when she says, "I am a silent red flag"?

Chapters 6–16: How does Cornelia react when people ask her why she doesn't talk?

Chapters 17–24: What did people tell Cornelia to do about her speech?

Chapters 25–36: While others have learned to speak for Cornelia, Agatha has not done this. Why?

Chapters 37–44: How do both Cornelia and Agatha feel like they have been "dumped"?

Chapters 45–64: How do Bo and Cornelia help each other?

Chapters 65–81: What do you think Agatha and Cornelia have been hiding from each other?

Chapters 82–89: How does the growth of the main characters compare to that of a butterfly?

Chapters 90–93: How does Cornelia prove that she is intelligent?

Chapters 94–83: How do Agatha and Cornelia "tend to Grace"?

Deafness and Hard of Hearing

Dad and Me in the Morning by Patricia Lakin (Robert G. Steele). 1994. Grade K+

A young boy is awakened by his special flashing alarm clock and joins his father for a walk to the beach. They like being together with no one else around. But most of all, they enjoy being together watching the colors of the clouds and sky change as the sun begins to rise over the horizon.

- Why does the boy call his alarm clock special?

- How do the boy and his father communicate with each other? Why?

- What do they see along the way to the beach?

- What different colors do they see in the sky?

- Have you ever seen a sunrise? How did it make you feel?

- Is there someone special you like to spend time with alone? Why?

Dad, Jackie, and Me by Myron Uhlberg (Colin Bootman). 2005. Grade 2+

A young Brooklyn Dodgers fan is excited that he and his father can finally see Jackie Robinson play in a major league baseball game. The boy's father is deaf and never learned to play baseball as a youth because he was considered severely disabled, and teaching sports was a waste of time. The boy learns how his father, like Jackie Robinson, persevered and succeeded regardless of discrimination.

- Why do you think the boy's father is interested in baseball?

- Why do you think the boy's father can't pronounce Jackie's name?

- How does Jackie Robinson react when a Giants fans taunts him?

- How is the boy's father a leader in speaking out against unfair treatment toward Jackie?

Deaf Child Crossing by Marlee Matlin. 2002. Grade 4+

Nine-year-old Megan is excited when Cindy and her family move into the neighborhood. Megan and Cindy quickly become friends, and Cindy learns sign language to communicate better with Megan, who is deaf. The girls go to summer camp, and Cindy feels left out when Megan starts to hang out with a girl who is deaf. The girls make up and start off the school year as best friends.

Chapters 1–2: Why does Cindy think that Megan had bubble gum in her ears?

Chapters 3–4: What does Cindy do to learn to communicate with Megan?

Chapters 5–7: Why do you think Megan doesn't want to go to camp?

Chapters 8–10: How is Megan surprised about Ruthie, the camp counselor?

Chapters 11–12: How did the girls make their camp cheer different from everyone else's?

Chapters 13–16: How is Cindy able to find Megan?

Chapters 17–19: Why do you think this book is titled *Deaf Child Crossing*? Why does the last chapter include a caution about a deaf child crossing?

Mandy by Barbara D. Booth (Jim Lamarche). 1991. Grade K+

Mandy and her grandmother spend the afternoon baking cookies, looking at family photos, and taking a walk. Mandy wonders about the sounds she cannot hear. Then she overcomes her fear of the dark to find her grandmother's lost pin during a storm.

- What do you think about Mandy putting a marshmallow to her ear to feel the "sweet softness of her mother's voice"?

- What different ways does Mandy use to communicate with her grandma?

- Why does Mandy think it is silly to stop dancing when a box decides rather than when you decide?

- How does Mandy use her senses to do her daily activities?

- How does Mandy use her senses to find her grandma's pin? Do you think her other senses are more sensitive since she can't hear? Why or why not?

Moses Goes to a Concert by Isaac Millman (Isaac Millman). 1998. Grade K+

Moses' class is going on a field trip to a young people's concert. All of Moses' classmates sit in the front row of the concert and hold balloons so they can feel the vibrations of the music because they are deaf or hard of hearing. Moses learns that he can become whatever he wants when he grows up.

- Can you feel the vibration of a drum through your hands? Through your feet? Through a balloon?

- Why do Moses and his classmates wave their hands instead of clap?

- What is the most important thing Moses learns from going to the concert?

Moses Sees a Play by Isaac Millman (Isaac Millman). 2004. Grade K+

Actors from the Little Theater of the Deaf put on a play at Moses' special school. They invite Ms. Morgan and her students, who are not deaf, to spend the day and see the play. Moses learns to communicate and become friends with Manuel, who does not know English or sign language yet.

- How does Moses communicate with Manuel?

- How are gestures similar to sign language?

- Why do you think this is the first live play many of the children have ever seen?

- What is a TTY? How does it work?

- Why do you think Manuel and Moses attend separate schools?

Nick's Mission by Claire H. Blatchford. 1994. Grade 4+

Nick, a sixth-grade student who is deaf, stops speaking to his mother to show his protest against attending speech therapy classes during his summer vacation. His mission to save the lake results in solving the dangerous case of the kidnapped scarlet macaws. Nick then realizes the importance of having the ability to speak and to understand people.

Chapters 1–2: How did Nick become deaf? How does he communicate with people? What does Nick do to avoid conversations that are unpleasant?

Chapters 3–4: Why is it important for Nick to see people's eyes?

Chapter 4: How does Nick communicate with his parents over the phone? How does Nick's mother respond to his no-talk plan?

Chapter 5: Why is it hard for Peter to believe that Nick could not sign or talk?

Chapter 6: What is Nick afraid will happen when he decides not to attend therapy classes?

Chapters 7–9: How does Nick understand Carlos's directions?

Chapter 10: What is Nick's reaction to a woman calling him "dumb"?

Chapters 11–13: Why does Peter think it is important for Nick to learn sign language?

Chapters 14–15: What does Nick learn about his intuition?

Nick's Secret by Claire H. Blatchford. 2000. Grade 4+

Nick, a boy who is deaf, is being bullied at school. When he rides out to an abandoned motel to confront his tormentors, he meets Ionie, a sixteen-year-old girl who needs his help. Nick has to decide whether he can keep Ionie and her problems a secret.

Chapters 1–2: Why is Nick so quick with his eyes? How does he communicate with others? How did Nick develop deafness? What is a TTY? How does it work?

Chapters 3–5: Does Nick make the right decision to meet Daryl instead of going to work on time? What would you have done?

Chapters 6–9: Why does Nick think his story seemed tame compared to Ionie's? Why won't Ionie go to the police? Do you agree with or understand her reason?

Chapters 10–11: Where does Nick tell his mother that he spent the night? Why doesn't he tell her the truth? Why do you think Nick's mom packed two of everything in his lunch?

Chapters 12–14: Why does Nick think Peter is scared of him? Do you think Nick will get a sheepdog? How do you think Wags will respond?

The Printer by Myron Uhlberg (Henri Sorensen). 2003. Grade 2+

A young boy tells the story of how his father works in a newspaper printing plant and is isolated from many of his coworkers because he is deaf. However, when a fire breaks out, this printer is able to save his fellow workers.

• Do you think the printer likes his job at the printing plant? Why or why not?

• Why do you think there were several workers at the printing plant who were deaf?

• How did the printer alert his coworkers of the fire? How did the use of sign language save their lives?

• How did the coworkers show their appreciation for the printer?

Emotional and Behavioral Disorders

Cut by Patricia McCormick. 2000. Grade 7+

Thirteen-year-old Callie is sent to a residential treatment facility because of her self-mutilation. Through interaction with other girls who have similar problems and treatment from the staff, she starts to understand why she cuts herself, and her healing process begins.

Chapter 1: Why do you think Callie has a difficult time speaking, even to her brother? In what way is not talking taking a lot of her energy? Why is Amanda so willing to show her scars, while Callie hides hers? Do you ever feel like withdrawing? When? What happens when you do? Why do you think Callie finally starts talking again?

Chapter 2: How would you describe the therapist's methods with Callie? Do you think Callie's mother really doesn't want her to be around? Why is Debbie always drawing pictures of thin women? Why do you think the girls at the facility are more observant of what each other does than the attendants are? What would you do if you saw someone break the rules? When does Callie get the urge to cut herself? Callie says everything wrong in her family is all her fault. Does that make sense to you? Why or why not?

Chapter 3: Why does Callie suddenly run away, and why does she want to return? Would you? In what ways has Callie's treatment helped her family? Will Callie be healed? Why or why not?

Heck Superhero by Martine Leavitt. 2004. Grade 6+

Thirteen-year-old Heck and his emotionally unstable mother are evicted from their apartment, and then she disappears. He searches for her for three days, trying to survive on his own but shifting between his imaginary superhero character and the harsh reality of his life.

Monday, May 2: Why won't Heck tell Spence and his parents about his predicament? Why does he take the pill? Would you? If you were a superhero, what would you call yourself? What words would be above your head in a bubble?

Tuesday, May 3: What is hypertime versus reality time? Why do you think Heck draws superheros instead of "artwork" when things get out of control? Why won't Heck tell Mr. Bandras about his situation?

Wednesday, May 4: How do you think Heck felt when the store clerk called him, "People like you"? How would you have felt? Heck thinks that for every good deed you do, you also get a good deed done to you. Do you agree? Why or why not?

Thursday, May 5: Do you think Marion has a mental illness? Why or why not? Why do you think Heck is so intent on painting Marion? Are you surprised by Marion's actions? Why or why not?

Friday, May 6: What does Heck conclude about good deeds? Do you agree? Why or why not? What do you think will happen to Heck and his mother?

📖 **I Am an Artichoke** by Lucy Frank. 1995. Grade 7+

As an escape from her boring suburban life, fifteen-year-old Sarah accepts a summer job as a "mother's helper" in New York City. She soon learns that she has been employed to help twelve-year-old Emily with a serious eating disorder.

Chapters 1–2: On what is the title of the book based? In what ways are all people "artichokes"?

Chapters 3–4: Why do you think Emily's mother hired a "companion" for Emily?

Chapters 5–6: Do Sarah and Emily go to the kitchen in the middle of the night for the same reason? Why are they so frightened Florence will discover what they've done?

Chapters 7–8: What does Emily mean when she says, "I eat what my body needs. I just don't stuff myself like a disgusting pig, that's all. That's what none of you understand"? Why doesn't Emily want to go back to a therapist?

Chapters 9–10: Why do you think Emily begins eating more? Do you agree with Florence's decision to talk about the exercise bicycle? Why or why not?

Chapters 11–12: What have you learned about Sarah and Emily thus far? Do you think they are truly friends? Why or why not?

Chapters 13–14: What does the cleaning crew find? Who do you think placed the items there? Why?

Chapters 15–16: Under what circumstances, if any, would it be appropriate for parents to read their child's diary? Do you think Florence's actions are appropriate? How is an eating disorder like a "power thing"?

Chapters 17–19: Why doesn't Emily think she looks as fat in Sarah's mirror as she does at home? Describe what you think will happen to Sarah and Emily in the next two years.

📖 **Inside Out** by Terry Trueman. 2003. Grade 9+

Zach, a sixteen-year-old with schizophrenia, finds himself in the wrong place at the wrong time and becomes a hostage in an attempted robbery by two other teens.

Chapters 1–3: How is Zach's schizophrenia manifested in these chapters? How would you characterize Frosty and Stormy?

Chapters 4–6: Why do you think the author starts each chapter with a transcript from Zach's past? Do you think it is an effective literary tool? What have you learned about Zach so far?

Chapters 7–9: What do you think Dr. Curt will do? Were Alan and Joey smart to solicit his help? Why or why not?

Chapters 10–13: Do you believe Alan and Joey are justified in robbing the store? Why or why not? How else could Alan and Joey have tried to get the money they needed?

Chapters 14–16: Have your feelings about Alan and Joey changed since the beginning of the book? If so, how and why?

Chapters 17–19: How are Alan and Joey like Zach? How are they different? Do you think Alan and Joey understand Zach's condition?

Chapters 20–23: Does the ending surprise you? How would you have ended the story? What have you learned about schizophrenia?

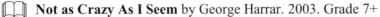 **Kissing Doorknobs** by Terry Spencer Hesser. 1998. Grade 7+

Fourteen-year-old Tara becomes obsessed with rituals that she cannot stop. They begin to take over her life and interfere with her relationships with family and friends.

Chapters 1–3: Over what things does Tara worry or fret? Do you have some of these same fears? In what ways are Tara's fears interfering with her life?

Chapters 4–7: Do you think Gretchen is justified in what she does? What would you have done if you were Tara or Gretchen in this situation?

Chapters 8–9: What ritual does Tara start in response to Tara's parents being gone at night? If you saw a friend doing this ritual, what would you think, say, and do?

Chapters 10–11: How does Tara's mother react to her rituals at the amusement park? Do you think she was justified? Why can't Tara just stop doing them?

Chapters 12–13: Why do you think Tara and Donna become friends? Do you think they are good for one another? Why or why not?

Chapters 14–16: How is Tara's behavior affecting her family? Why do you think the doctors don't know what is really wrong with her?

Chapters 17–18: Who is it that finally explains what is wrong with Tara? Explain what's meant by Tara's brain hiccupping. How does Tara react to knowing others have her problem?

Chapters 19–20: What is behavior therapy? Do you think it will work for Tara?

Chapters 21–23: What role reversal happens in these chapters? What will Tara and Sam's lives be like and what kind of relationship will Tara and Sam have in the next three years?

Not as Crazy As I Seem by George Harrar. 2003. Grade 7+

Fifteen-year-old Devon is fixated on the number four and obsessed about germs and untidiness, all of which have troubled him since his grandfather's death when he was eight. When Devon's parents decide to move, he must adjust to a new private school and a new therapist.

Chapters 1–2: How would you describe Devon? Why do you think Devon sees a therapist?

Chapters 3–5: What unusual things does Devon do on his first day of school? If you saw a new student do these things, what would you think about him or her?

Chapters 6–9: Devon tells his therapist, "I wasn't wrong, really. I just did something that *seems* wrong. There's a big difference." Do you agree? Why or why not?

Chapters 10–12: Will Devon and Ben become friends? If so, will it be good for Devon? Why or why not?

Chapters 13–16: What do you think about Devon's self-esteem tapes? Will they help Devon? Would you use them? Why or why not?

Chapters 17–19: Is Devon as guilty as Ben? Why or why not?

Chapters 20–23: Why do you think Devon won't tell on Ben? Would you?

Chapter 24–Epilogue: What have you learned about obsessive-compulsive disorder in these chapters? What do you think the future holds for Devon?

📖 **The Planet of Junior Brown** by Virginia Hamilton. 1971. Grade 7+, Newbery Honor Book
Junior and Buddy, two African American teenagers, spend their school days in a secret cellar room with the help of the school janitor—a former teacher whose model solar system in the room becomes a haven for the boys. As Junior struggles with obesity, a deteriorating family life, and the loss of music in his life, Buddy, a boy with his own problems, comes to Junior's aid.

Chapter 1: What do you think motivates Buddy and Mr. Pool to keep trying to help Junior? What keeps Junior from taking full advantage of the situation?

Chapter 2: Why is Junior so helpless about his weight? How do eating disorders compare to other disabilities and diseases?

Chapter 3: How has secrecy affected relationships between the various characters? How might Junior's eating disorder symbolize or result from the other problems he faces?

Chapter 4: In what ways are Junior's home life and Buddy's planet similar? How might these similarities draw them together?

Chapter 5: How might overeating be an attempt to fill a void in Junior's life? How do you generally deal with such voids?

Chapter 6: How is the Planet of Junior Brown (in the school solar system) symbolic? Given that it is brought to life by "themselves and how they felt about one another," what is the significance of its death?

Chapter 7: What made Junior go crazy, and why was the planet able to bring him out of it? In retrospect, where did Junior's eating disorder fit in relation to his other problems? How might his new life on the planet affect his disorder?

📖 **Reaching Dustin** by Vicki Grove. 1998. Grade 5+
After Carly is assigned to interview the class bully, Dustin, for a class project, she is startled by what she learns about his home life. She discovers that a childish prank she pulled against him years ago has contributed to his antisocial behavior.

Chapters 1–2: How would you feel if you'd been assigned to interview Dustin?

Chapters 3–5: What has Carly learned about Dustin? Why do you think she's so persistent when he appears so resistant?

Chapters 6–7: Describe Dustin's house and yard. Would you like to live there? Why or why not?

Chapters 8–9: Carly tells Luke the "Goatboy" that he is not nice because he doesn't want to be nice. Do you agree? Why or why not?

Chapters 10–11: What does "walking in someone else's shoes" really mean?

Chapters 12–14: Why does Dustin look so different in the woods? Describe someone in your life who might look different in different settings.

Chapters 15–16: What does Dustin ask Carly? Do you think Carly really remembers that day?

Chapters 17–18: How do you think Dustin hurt his arm? Do you agree with Luke that Caralotta was mean to the Goatboy? Why or why not?

Chapters 19–21: What do you think caused the slimy, yellowish-brown and red ooze?

Chapters 22–23: What does Carly mean when she says that writing is like taking an exciting trip, but sometimes it takes you on detours to places you don't want to go?

Chapters 24–27: What do you think of Carly's essay? What will happen when Dustin goes to the school board?

The Tulip Touch by Anne Fine. 1997. Grade 6+

Natalie, who has moved into a large hotel run by her father, befriends Tulip, a girl who likes to play bullying and dangerous games. When they burn a shed, Natalie becomes scared and realizes that she can no longer be Tulip's friend.

Chapters 1–3: Would you like to live in Natalie's hotel? Why or why not?

Chapters 4–6: Why do you think Natalie is so drawn to Tulip even at the expense of not playing with other girls? Have you ever felt that way about a friend?

Chapters 7–9: What exactly is the "Tulip touch?" Provide some examples.

Chapters 10–12: If you were Natalie, would you go along with the games? Why or why not? Why do you think Tulip turns on Natalie?

Chapters 13–14: Does Natalie really want to go to Heathcote? Would you? Why or why not?

Chapters 15–18: Why do you think Natalie continues to be Tulip's friend? What other choices does she have?

Chapters 19–21: What does Tulip's self-portrait tell us about her?

Chapters 22–23: Explain why Natalie says that she had to think poorly of Tulip to save her own life. How do you think Tulip will react to not being invited to Natalie's house for Christmas?

Chapters 24–26: Do you think Tulip's behavior gets worse because Natalie is no longer her friend? How hard do you think it was for Natalie to be friendless?

Chapters 27–30: In the first chapter Natalie tells the reader that she isn't certain the story is over. What do you think she means?

When She Was Good by Norma Fox Mazer. 1997. Grade 8+

After her physically and emotionally abusive mentally ill older sister dies, Em recalls their times together and begins her first steps toward liberation.

Chapters 1–5: Why do you think Em continues to hear her sister's voice? What is symbolic about having two funerals?

Chapters 6–10: In what ways does the family trailer look different from how Em remembered it? Has that ever happened to you? When and where?

Chapters 11–14: In what way is Pamela like a "planet rocketing along in a parallel universe?" What about Em? Do you think their father's abuse contributed to their emotional problems? How?

Chapters 15–22: How do Pamela and Em's world change when their father remarries? Do you think Pamela and Em made the right decision to leave their house? Why or why not? What does the future hold for the two living on their own?

Chapters 23–29: Why do you think Em kept thinking things would turn out all right if she was good? Who is William? How would you describe him?

Chapters 30–37: Why do you think Em cannot rid herself of Pamela? Why is Em so attracted to the dark-haired woman?

Chapters 38–43: What is significant about Em finally finding the apartment empty and then finding a job?

Chapters 44–50: How is the relationship between Em and Lana similar to and different than Em and Louise's relationship? How many minutes do you think passed before Em called 911? How is Em's life like elderberry jam?

Intellectual Disability

Be Good to Eddie Lee by Virginia Fleming (Floyd Cooper). 1993. Grade K+
Christy thinks Eddie Lee, a boy with Down syndrome, is a pest until he shows her some special discoveries she has never seen before in the woods.

- Why does Christy's mom tell her to be good to Eddie Lee?

- How would you feel if someone called you "dummy?"

- What does Eddie Lee show Christy? What does she call him?

- Would you like to be Eddie Lee's friend? Why?

Because of Winn-Dixie by Kate DiCamillo. 2000. Grade 3+, Newbery Honor Book
Ten-year-old Opal and her preacher father move to Florida, where she adopts a big ugly dog, whom she names Winn-Dixie. Because of Winn-Dixie, Opal makes friends with other lonely people, including Otis, who is considered slow. Opal learns a lot about her mother, who abandoned them seven years ago.

Chapters 1–3: What would you have named Winn-Dixie and why?

Chapters 4–6: What ten things would you tell someone about a member of your family?

Chapters 7–10: How would you describe Miss Fanny, Otis, and Gloria? How are they similar? How are they different?

Chapters 11–12: Why do you think Winn-Dixie is afraid of thunderstorms? What do Opal and Sweetie Pie call Otis? Why?

Chapters 13–15: Stevie calls Otis "retarded." Do you think Otis has mental retardation? Why or why not? What does Gloria teach Opal about judging other people?

Chapters 16–19: What do the Littmus Lozenges taste like? What ingredients would make them taste this way?

Chapters 20–22: Do you think the party will be ruined by the rain? Why or why not?

Chapters 23–26: What does Opal learn about her mother, her father, and herself by the end of the book?

Ben, King of the River by David Gifaldi (Layne Johnson). 2001. Grade K+
Chad goes camping with his family and is embarrassed by his younger brother's behavior. But when Ben, the five-year-old brother with a developmental disability, makes friends with other campers who had made fun of him earlier, Chad realizes that his brother is not so bad.

- Why does Ben's behavior worry Chad?

- What are some of the things Ben does well?

- What would you do if someone was making fun of your brother?

- Why is Ben called "King of the River?"

The Best Worst Brother by Stephanie Stuve-Bodeen (Charlotte Fremaux). 2005. Grade K+

Three-year-old Isaac, who has Down syndrome, is being taught sign language by his family. His older sister, Emma, works hard to make him understand. He does learn, although at a slower pace than she would like. This is a sequel to *We'll Paint the Octopus Red*.

- How is Isaac different now that he has grown up?

- How does Isaac's sister try to help him?

- Why does Isaac's sister get frustrated with Isaac?

- Why do you think Miss Becker understands the way Isaac behaves?

The Bus People by Rachel Anderson. 1992. Grade 5+

Each chapter profiles one of the passengers that Bertram, the "special bus" driver, transports to and from school each day. These include Andy, who has muscular dystrophy; Rebecca, who has Down syndrome; Micky, who has intellectual and orthopedic disabilities; Jonathan, who has an intellectual disability; Marilyn, who has microcephaly, intellectual, and orthopedic disabilities; Fleur, who has a communication disorder and emotional and intellectual disabilities; Thoby, who experienced a traumatic brain injury; and Danny, who has an intellectual disability.

Chapter 1: Why are Bertram and Andy's family so taken with these children with disabilities? Do you know anyone with health problems like Andy's? What are the implications of possibly having a seizure at any time?

Chapter 2: What does Rebecca hold onto more than anything else? Why is it such an important anchor for her?

Chapter 3: How has Mickey's overly sheltered life affected his perception of reality? How accurately do Mickey's physical capabilities represent his intellectual abilities?

Chapter 4: What does it take for Jonathan finally to have a chance to feel useful? Is he useful? Why should we value the contributions of those with disabilities?

Chapter 5: What makes Marilyn "see the world differently"? What seems to be the root of it? From what you know of Fleur, why do you suppose she doesn't like to speak?

Chapter 6: How does the chapter suggest we can come to accept and appreciate those with disabilities? What enables Thoby to begin to learn things for himself?

Chapter 7: Compare your own learning style to Danny's. Why do people learn in such different ways? Why is it helpful to include people with a variety of strengths and experiences? How can the attitudes of peers and teachers affect a student's chances for success?

Chapter 8: Put yourself in Bertram's shoes. How would you have responded to this situation? What have you learned about people with disabilities from this book? How have your attitudes about these individuals changed, if at all?

Crazy Lady by Jane Leslie Conly. 1993. Grade 5+, Newbery Honor Book

In danger of having to repeat the seventh grade, Vernon Dibbs reluctantly accepts help from an English tutor, Miss Annie. When Miss Annie asks him to pay for his tutoring by helping the "Crazy Lady" and Ronald, her son with intellectual disabilities, Vernon does so grudgingly. Eventually Vernon becomes friends with Ronald, bringing the community together to send him to the Special Olympics.

Chapters 1–2: What does Vernon's mother think of children who "keep on trying, even when it's hard?"

Chapters 3–4: Why do the neighborhood kids call Maxine "Crazy Lady"? How could they have found out "all about her" in a more appropriate way?

Chapters 5–6: What does Vernon do to improve his reading and spelling?

Chapters 7–8: What attributes does Vernon discover in Ronald during their hour together without Maxine?

Chapters 9–12: How does Vernon's willingness to befriend Ronald influence his friends and community?

Chapters 13–18: If Ronald "knows more than he lets on," why would he choose to hide it?

Chapters 19–27: What positive aspects does Ronald's family contribute to his well-being? How might your community treat parents whom they deem to be unfit parents?

Chapters 28–30: When does Ronald first try to say the word "dog"? How does Vernon feel? Why do you think Ronald doesn't say "dog" later when he was at home? Do you think it is possible to learn even if you can't speak? Why or why not?

Chapters 31–32: How do you think life will be different for Ronald in North Carolina?

Dustin's Big School Day by Alden R. Carter (Dan Young and Carol S. Carter). 1999. Grade K+

Dustin, who has Down syndrome, is excited about the special event planned for later in the school day, when a family friend, Dave, a ventriloquist, and Skippy, his talking puppet, visit Dustin's school.

• Why do you think Dustin is excited about school today?

• How is Dustin a good friend?

• What types of classes does Dustin attend at school? Which subjects are the same as what you learn? Which are different?

• How do the children respond to Dave and Skippy's visit?

Keeping Up with Roo by Sharlee Glenn (Dan Andreasen). 2004. Grade K+, Dolly Gray Award

When Gracie was young, her Aunt Roo, who is depicted as having intellectual disabilities, was her best friend. She played with Gracie and taught her to walk, count, and read. When Gracie begins school and brings home a new friend, she ignores Roo, but eventually remembers how special Roo is to her and includes her in their activities.

- How did Roo help Gracie when she was a baby? How did she help her when she was a young child?

- What fun things do you like to do with your aunt, if you have one?

- Why does Gracie take over the teacher's desk when she is in second grade?

- How do you think Roo felt when Gracie stopped playing with her?

- Why does Gracie change her mind about including Roo in their activities?

- How is Gracie keeping up with Roo?

Me and Rupert Goody by Barbara O'Connor. 1999. Grade 4+, Dolly Gray Award

Jennalee is content with her predictable life helping a kind old man known as "Uncle Beau" in the town's general store. When Uncle Beau's illegitimate, intellectually challenged, part African American son suddenly appears on the scene, Jennalee must learn to look beyond the surface and accept Rupert as part of her life.

Chapters 1–3: Why doesn't Jennalee like Rupert?

Chapters 4–5: Uncle Beau tells Jennalee that "sometimes what's in a heart means . . . more than what's in a head." How might this apply to Rupert? What about other people you know?

Chapters 6–7: Why is Rupert so kind to Jennalee, even though she doesn't like him?

Chapters 8–9: Why do you think the storm and the accident with Uncle Beau scare Rupert?

Chapters 10–11: Jennalee told Rupert that he made Uncle Beau sick. What makes this a bad thing to say to Rupert?

Chapters 12–13: What terms should we avoid using when referring to individuals with mental retardation? Why?

Chapters 14–15: What does Jennalee mean when she says that she and Rupert "had a lot in common"?

My Louisiana Sky by Kimberly Willis Holt. 1998. Grade 6+

Twelve-year old Tiger Ann Parker lives in a small town with her intellectually "slow" parents, and her grandmother, who holds the family together. Caught between trying to fit in with her peers and helping care for her family, Tiger is left helpless when her grandmother suddenly dies. When her "sophisticated" aunt from Baton Rouge offers her a home in the city, away from the teasing and the heartache, Tiger must decide who she really is and what matters most.

Chapters 1–3: How do you think her parents' disabilities have affected Tiger's personality? Are they affecting her desire to change her identity now?

Chapters 4–5: Do you believe Tiger's mother is as unintelligent as Tiger seems to believe? How would you help Tiger see her mother in a more positive light?

Chapters 6–7: Have you ever been afraid of someone or something different? How can we learn to accept and appreciate people's differences?

Chapters 8–10: How could the family have better prepared for life without Granny? Why is it important that persons with disabilities learn independent living skills?

Chapters 11–13: What do you think of Tiger's aunt's invitation to move to Baton Rouge? What do you think will be best for Tiger? For her family?

Chapters 14–16: What is different about the way Magnolia treats Tiger's parents?

Chapters 17–18: How is Magnolia able to bring Momma out of her grieving?

Chapters 19–20: What brings about Tiger's change in attitude toward her mother? Why does Tiger decide to stay in Saitter? Do you agree with her decision? Explain.

Russ and the Almost Perfect Day by Janet Elizabeth Rickert (Pete McGahan). 2001. Grade K+

Russ, a boy with Down syndrome, is having a great day, especially when he finds money on the way to school. When he is ready to use the money to buy ice cream, he sees a girl crying because she lost her lunch money. Russ then gives her the bill he found.

- Why do you think Russ decides to keep the money he found?

- What events made the school day seem to be "almost perfect"? How could the day have truly been "perfect"?

- What would you have done if you were Russ? Would you give the money to the girl, even if you didn't know whether it belonged to her?

So B. It by Sarah Weeks. 2004. Grade 6+, Dolly Gray Award
Twelve-year-old Heidi lives with her mother who has intellectual disabilities, and Bernadette, a neighbor with agoraphobia, or fear of being in public places. Heidi ventures from Reno, Nevada, to Liberty, New York, in search of who she really is. In the end, she is liberated by her discovery about her family history.

Chapters 1–3: "All not knowing something means is that there's still room left to wonder." What does that mean? Who has and what is agoraphobia?

Chapters 4–6: How would you feel if someone called you a "retard"? What would you do? What do you think "soof" means?

Chapters 7–9: What does "get a life" mean to Judi? What does it mean to Heidi?

Chapters 10–12: Do you agree that "certain things that seem to happen by accident don't really happen by accident at all?" Why or why not?

Chapters 13–15: Why does Thurman Hill know Mama's word? What do you think he is covering up?

Chapters 16–19: How is Heidi's life like the jar of jelly beans? Do you agree that there are some things in life a person just can't know?

Chapters 20–21: Why do you think Sophia and Elliot never married?

Chapters 22–23: Why do you think the author titled Chapter 22, "Done"? What did "soof" mean to Mama?

Sparks by Graham McNamee. 2002. Grade 4+
Ten-year-old Todd Foster has been promoted from a fourth-grade "Special Needs" class to "the real fifth grade." Todd, who is described as a "slow learner," is afraid that he will not succeed in a general classroom. While struggling with maintaining friendships with classmates in his special education class, he tries to be accepted by his nondisabled peers in the fifth grade.

Chapters 1–2: How does Todd feel about leaving the "Special Needs" class so he can have a "trial period" in fifth grade?

Chapters 3–4: Do you think it's fair for Mr. Blaylock to suggest to Todd that if in four weeks he can't prove himself, that he will be sent back to the Special Needs class? Is this legal?

Chapters 5–6: Do you think there is truth to Todd's statement, "That's the thing about being slow, even when you're right nobody believes you"? Why or why not?

Chapters 7–9: Todd is afraid to let Mr. Blaylock know that he "is lost" with some of his work. Do you ever worry about letting people know when you are confused?

Chapters 10–11: Todd describes his feelings about attending school as like being on a deserted island or falling off a cliff. Why do you think he is feeling this way? Do you think it is better for him to feel secure and "smart" in the Special Needs class or to feel challenged in the general classroom?

Chapters 12–18: How does Todd feel about being called "Mr. Retardo," "Brain Dead," and "Gump"? Do you ever hear kids call each other names like this? How do you think it makes them feel?

Chapters 19–23: How do you think Todd and Ota Benga are similar and different?

Chapters 24–27: How did Todd show that he had "smart sparks"?

📖 **Summer of the Swans** by Betsy Byars. 1970. Grade 4+, Newbery Medal Book

Sara has the "most terrible summer ever" and is changed by the disappearance of her brother, Charlie, who has an intellectual disability. When Sara finds Charlie alone in a ravine and frightened by the unfamiliarity of his surroundings, she no longer finds her own concerns so weighty, having gained greater appreciation for her brother.

Chapters 1–2: Sara measures her self-worth by comparing her appearance with that of others. How might this contribute to the worst summer of her life?

Chapters 3–5: What does Wanda mean when she tells Sara that Charlie is everybody's problem? What, if any, responsibility do we have for other people's problems?

Chapters 6–8: What do you think the swans symbolize? What do you think the author means when she describes the swans as "painfully beautiful"? Why do you think Charlie refuses to leave the swans?

Chapters 9–12: Why does Charlie go after the swans? What was he really chasing? How could the other characters in the story have helped to meet those needs? How will Sara react to Charlie's disappearance?

Chapters 13–14: Sara confronts Joe Melby about stealing Charlie's watch. How does the situation end differently than she had planned? Why does Sara react to this encounter the way she did?

Chapters 15–16: Do you think Sara really understands Charlie's feelings? If so, what does this say about the similarities between those with and without disabilities?

Chapters 17–18: How is Sara's search for Charlie similar to Charlie's search for the swans?

Chapters 19–20: Sara compares her previous troubles to her present worry. Why might this problem be a "true sadness" compared with her earlier struggles?

Chapters 21–23: What do you think of Sara's staircase analogy? How might people progress or regress along the staircase of life? Why are the steps different for everyone? Does everyone have the ability to progress?

📖 **Tru Confessions** by Janet Tashjian. 1997. Grade 4+, Dolly Gray Award

Twelve-year-old Trudy (known as Tru) has two primary ambitions in life: to produce her own television show and to cure her brother of his intellectual disability. Writing in her electronic diary, Tru reveals her hopes, fears, and feelings of incompetence. When she receives helpful feedback from an unknown electronic email buddy (which happens to be her mother), Tru learns that she doesn't need to cure her brother and that she can still attain some of her dreams. *Note: The chapters in this book are not numbered. For convenience, we list the questions and corresponding chapters in their numerical order.*

Chapters 1–12: How does Tru feel about having a twin brother with a disability?

Chapters 13–16: Why do you think Tru wants to cure her brother?

Chapters 17–22: How is Eddie like a "walking meditation"?

Chapters 23–32: Do you think Tru feels guilty for causing Eddie's disability? Is this the reason she is producing a TV show about him?

Chapters 33–40: Although Tru has made fun of Eddie in the past, she doesn't allow others to bully him. Why do you think she is such a strong protector of her brother?

Chapters 41–43: When Eddie has a panic attack in the mall he told Tru, "I don't want to be different." Tru assured him that "Everybody is different . . . Not just you." Do you think Tru really believes this? Why or why not?

Chapters 44–48: Tru has a fear of being developmentally delayed. Is this a realistic or unrealistic fear?

Chapters 49–51: How is Eddie like "one special tulip"? Can anyone else be considered a special tulip?

Chapters 52–56: Why was Tru upset with the reaction she received about her show?

Chapters 57–60: Do you think Tru realized that "deedee" was her mother? Is it sometimes easier to discuss sensitive issues while being anonymous?

We'll Paint the Octopus Red by Stephanie Stuve-Bodeen (Pam DeVito). 1998. Grade K+
When Emma learns that her parents are going to have a new baby, she plans some of the things they will do together—including painting a plastic octopus at the art festival. When the baby is born, Emma's father tells her that Isaac has Down syndrome and that it might take him longer to learn to do things than other kids. Emma learns that she can still do all of the things that she was planning to do with Isaac.

- How does Emma feel when she finds out that her mom is going to have a baby?

- What are some of the things that Emma wants to show the baby?

- How is baby Isaac different than other babies? How is he the same?

- What is Down syndrome?

- What did Emma find out that she could do with Isaac?

Learning Disabilities

The Alphabet War by Diane Burton Robb (Gail Piazza). 2004. Grade K+
Adam, initially excited about learning to read, slowly loses interest and becomes frustrated as he falls farther and farther behind his class. Adam sees reading as an "alphabet war." Soon, a special education team discovers Adam's dyslexia and helps him learn to compensate and begin to read on his own.

- Why is learning to read so hard for Adam?

- What does it mean to be "a different kind of thinker"?

- How should we act when our friends have a hard time learning things?

- What changes Adam's mind about himself?

- How can you be like Adam and try to get better at things that are hard for you?

Dicey's Song by Cynthia Voigt. 1982. Grade 6+, Newbery Medal Book

Dicey and her three siblings, including Maybeth who has a learning disability, move in with their grandmother because their mother is in a psychiatric institution. Dicey becomes the glue that keeps the family together. Through a series of struggles, including their mother's death, the family buries old fears and begins to heal.

Chapters 1–2: How might Dicey's sailboat symbolize her family's situation? What is the significance of her reaction to the sailboat sinking? What does it mean to be "retarded"? What is an appropriate way to refer to those with intellectual disabilities?

Chapters 3–4: Why was it important that Gram allow Maybeth to take piano lessons? Why does she learn music so much more quickly than reading? How should the school have handled Maybeth's difficulties?

Chapters 5–6: How have Maybeth's struggles in reading helped improve the family's relationships? Why would James pretend to be less smart than he is?

Chapters 7–8: How is "reaching out" related to "holding on?" What does Gram mean when she says, "You don't go reaching out with your hand closed up?" How has Maybeth's personality changed, and why?

Chapters 9–10: What makes Dicey suddenly want to take Momma home with them? How can you let go of something and still remember it?

Chapters 11–12: Compare the last sentence of the book to the first sentence of the book. Why would the author begin with an ending and end with a beginning? How have each of the Tillermans (and the family overall) changed over the course of the book? What things might have contributed to these changes?

Freak the Mighty by Rodman Philbrick. 1993. Grade 6+

Max, an oversized eighth grader with learning disabilities, and Kevin, his undersized classmate with orthopedic impairments, join strengths to become "Freak the Mighty." When Max's paroled father kidnaps him, the real power of Freak the Mighty is put to the test.

Chapters 1–2: Why do you think Max sees himself as unintelligent?

Chapters 3–4: Why are Freak and Max able to make friends so easily? What common stereotypes does Gwen manifest in her initial fear of Max?

Chapters 5–7: What does the term "retard" mean? What terms might we appropriately use when speaking of those with disabilities? How are Max and Freak more "able" than the gang?

Chapters 8–9: Based on Max's description of his disability, what challenges might he face in school? From Freak's "bionic dream," what insights can we gain about the similarities between those with disabilities and those without?

Chapters 10–11: Why does Max find references to "poor Kevin" offensive? How can focusing on differences further ostracize those with disabilities from society?

Chapters 12–13: What are "accommodations," and how does Mrs. Donelli use them to help Max succeed?

Chapters 14–15: Why is the dictionary Freak gives Max more special to him than his other presents? What was Freak trying to say by giving it to Max? Why did Freak's reaction to his present have such an effect on Max?

Chapters 16–18: Why would Mr. Kane say, "You can't trust a cripple?" What causes people to associate physical ability with moral stature?

Chapters 19–21: What is significant about the name "Freak the Mighty?"

Chapters 22–23: Why does Kevin have such confidence that Max can write the story despite his disability?

Chapters 24–25: Why doesn't Dr. Spivak see Kevin's story as a lie? How would you answer Max's question, "What does it really matter if we're all going to die in the end?" Why does Loretta's statement that "nothing is a drag" help Max start moving forward again?

📖 **The Hard Life of Seymour E. Newton** by Ann Bixby Herold. 1990. Grade 2+

Peter, a third-grade student with a learning disability, stays home with the flu for several days and watches a spider build a web outside his bedroom window. When his mother sweeps the corners of the window and breaks the web, Peter becomes upset. His discovery of the spider's return coincides with his own return to school and commitment to not get discouraged when he does not at first succeed.

Chapters 1–2: Why do you think Peter doesn't pass his spelling test?

Chapters 3–4: What kind of doctor is Dr. Kelly? What does he do with Peter? What learning tools do Peter and Craig use? Why are they called tools?

Chapters 5–6: How does Peter react to those teasing him? What do you do when people tease you?

Chapters 7–8: Who is Seymour E. Newton? Have you ever made up a name for something?

Chapters 9–10: Why did Peter open the window and break the spider web? Did it do any good?

Chapters 11–12: How does Peter help his dad? Have you ever helped your parents like this? What does Peter learn from his dad?

Chapters 13–15: What does Peter decide to build? Why? What does Peter learn about Nancy that surprises him? Why does Peter change his mind about Ed?

Chapters 16–17: Why does everyone look "Monday-morning tired" on the bus? What does that mean? What has Peter learned from Seymour? What have you learned from Peter?

How Many Days Until Tomorrow? by Caroline Janover. 2000. Grade 4+

Josh, who has learning disabilities, and his gifted brother spend some time living with their grandparents on an island off the coast of Maine. Josh struggles getting along with and appreciating his gruff grandfather, until an accident occurs.

Chapters 1–3: Will John have an enjoyable summer on the island? Why or why not?

Chapters 4–6: How do you think Josh feels when his grandfather keeps correcting him? Where do you think the title of the book comes from?

Chapters 7–9: What does Josh do to find his way home when he gets lost on the island? What would you have done?

Chapters 10–12: Why do you think Josh is always mixing up the letters in words? Do you know anyone who has these difficulties?

Chapters 13–15: Why does Josh decide to stay? Will he be glad he made this decision?

Chapters 16–18: How does Josh feel when he ruins his castle? Is it worth it to help his grandfather?

Chapters 19–21: How has the accident changed Gramps and his relationship with Josh? Will Josh and his brother return to stay on the island again?

I Got a "D" in Salami by Henry Winkler and Lin Oliver. 2003. Grade 4+ (Hank Zipzer Series #2)

While avoiding showing his report card to his parents, Hank's report card gets ground up in his mom's soy salami at the deli. Hank must rescue the salami before it gets eaten at a party. Hank finally gets testing for help in school with his learning challenges.

Chapters 1–3: Do you think Hank will spell his words correctly? Why or why not? Have you ever felt like Hank feels? When?

Chapters 4–6: Why do you think Hank can suddenly spell the word "separate" correctly to Mrs. Crock?

Chapters 7–8: Why does Hank believe he deserves the "lousy grades" he got?

Chapters 9–11: Do you think it was smart to destroy Hank's report card? Will Hank's parents still find out about the grades he earned?

Chapters 12–13: What does Hank mean by having something on your mind versus under it? Do you think making a minute-by-minute plan is a good idea? Why or why not?

Chapters 14–16: Why does Hank call himself stupid? How would you feel if you were Hank? What does Papa Pete teach Hank about lying?

Chapters 17–19: What do you think will happen to Hank Zipzer?

Chapters 20–22: How do Hank's feelings about being tested change? Why?

Chapters 23–24: What does Hank learn about himself in the meeting? Describe how Hank's homework chart will work.

Chapters 25–26: What does Hank give Mr. Gistediano? Why? What does Hank's father mean when he says Hank has brought his grades way up?

Life Magic by Melrose Cooper. 1996. Grade 4+

Sixth-grade Crystal struggles in school. Being the middle child between two gifted sisters doesn't help. Uncle Joe moves in with her family because he has AIDS and his health is deteriorating. Crystal and Joe become close, particularly after he tells her he also had problems learning in school.

Chapters 1–2: What do you think Crystal means by "The reading part was okay with me. It was the finding out what's what that had me scared"?

Chapters 3–4: Why is the family so excited to learn Uncle Joe is coming to stay with them?

Chapters 5–6: How is picking up someone from the airport different today than it was at the time portrayed in the story? Why is it different?

Chapters 7–8: Why do you think the author named the book *Life Magic*?

Chapters 9–10: Explain what Crystal means by "remedial reading class was being like the cold not being so bad when Uncle Joe and I made snow angels."

Chapters 11–12: Do you think Crystal was justified in how she treated Lamar? Why or why not?

Chapters 13–14: How is Crystal "all fizzed out like a soda bottle"?

Chapters 15–16: What are some other examples of irony that happen in the book? What about in your life?

Chapters 17–18: Why does Crystal finally feel like writing in her journal? Do you keep a journal? If so, what do you write about?

Chapters 19–20: Why do you think it took Crystal so long to grieve for her uncle?

Chapters 21–22: What kind of "abracadabra" things have happened in your life?

My Name Is ~~Brain~~ Brian by Jeanne Betancourt. 1993. Grade 4+

Brian loves hanging out with his best friends—Dan, John, and Richie, all members of the Jokers' Club. None of them are looking forward to school starting again—particularly Brian, who has problems with academic work. His new teacher, however, helps identify Brian's learning disability and he gets the help he needs.

Chapters 1–2: Why does Brian chant "I can do it" over and over before his first day at school? Why are the boys surprised by their teacher?

Chapters 3–4: How do you think Isabel feels when they call her an ape? How would you treat Isabelle? What does Mr. Bigham tell Brian's parents? How can people be smart in different ways? What does Brian do in the resource room?

Chapters 5–6: Why is Brian embarrassed about the tape recorder in class? Who does Brian see at the clubhouse? Why is he surprised?

Chapters 7–8: Why does Brian feel his friends are turning on him? What does Brian learn about his grandfather? How do John and Richie trick Brian and Dan? Was that fair? Why do you think they believed them?

Chapters 9–10: What does Brian learn about his father? Why do you think Isabel decided to change her appearance?

Chapters 11–12: Can people ever "get over" being dyslexic? Do you think Brian was happy that school was over?

Niagara Falls, or Does It? by Henry Winkler and Lin Oliver. 2003. Grade 4+ (Hank Zipzer Series #1)

After being called to the principal's office on the first day of school, Hank's fourth-grade experience seems to be getting worse, until the music teacher recognizes his learning difficulties and suggests that he be tested.

Chapters 1–2: Why do you think it's hard for Hank to write one good sentence?

Chapters 3–4: How are Hank and Frankie alike? How are they different?

Chapters 5–6: Who is Papa Pete, and why does Hank love him so much? How is Hank greeted when he arrives home?

Chapters 7–8: Where is the clubhouse? What does Hank decide to do for his essay? Do you think his teacher will agree with his decision?

Chapters 9–10: Do you think Hank's Niagara Falls will work? Which is your favorite thing that Hank thinks will happen after others see his project? Why?

Chapters 11–14: What could Hank have done to prevent the disaster? What punishment do you think Hank deserves?

Chapters 15–16: What made Hank feel good about school?

Chapters 17–18: Why is Mr. Rock different from other teachers? What does he recommend to Hank's parents?

Chapters 19–20: How would you describe the magic show? What did Papa Pete teach Hank?

Summer School! What Genius Thought That Up? by Henry Winkler and Lin Oliver. 2005. Grade 4+ (Henry Zipzer Series #8)

Hank Zipzer doesn't think it's fair that he has to go to summer school while his friends and sister attend Junior Explorers and have fun. It turns out, however, that Hank also has fun and learns a few things along the way.

Chapters 1–3: Why does Hank need to go to summer school? How does Hank feel when Nick calls him a dummy?

Chapters 4–6: Do you think it's fair that Hank has to go to summer school instead of Junior Explorers? What kind of learning challenge does Hank have?

Chapters 7–8: Whom does Hank meet at recess? What impresses Hank about this person?

Chapters 9–10: Why is Hank upset that Frankie and Ashley are doing a magic trick for the talent show? How would you feel? If you were in a Hawaiian talent show, what would you do?

Chapters 11–13: Why does Hank think Mr. Rock thought he'd be interested in Albert Einstein? Who would you choose to write about in a school report?

Chapters 14–16: How does Hank prepare for his report? What did Hank do for the first time? Why is he so excited? What is Hank's rule? Would his rule help you?

Chapters 17–18: Why do you think Hank's father wouldn't change his mind?

Chapters 19–21: How did Hank feel at the end of the chapter? Have you ever felt this way? When?

Chapters 22–24: How did Mason help Hank with his grade? Why does Hank think this is the greatest day of his life? What is the greatest day of your life so far? Why?

Thank You, Mr. Falker by Patricia Polacco (Patricia Polacco). 1998. Grade K+

Trisha is excited to start school so she can learn to read. By first grade, however, she becomes frustrated with how easy reading seems for everyone but her. She is teased incessantly. Finally, Mr. Falker, her fifth-grade teacher, comes to the rescue.

- What does Trisha like to do in school? What do you like to do?

- What is hard for Trisha? What is hard for you?

- How does Trisha feel when she is called dumb?

- How would you treat Trisha if you were in her class?

- Why did the author title this book *Thank You, Mr. Falker*?

- How are the author and Trisha related?

Whittington by Alan Armstrong. 2005. Grade 4+, Newbery Honor Book

Whittington, a battered tomcat, is gradually welcomed by the other barn animals. When winter arrives and all the animals are bored, Whittington begins telling stories about his namesake, Dick Whittington. Ben, a young boy with learning disabilities, and his sister, Abby, soon become part of the audience, and the animals' influence extends to helping Ben learn to read.

Chapters 1–5: In what ways does buying the horses help Bernie's family? How do you think Whittington will help Bernie's family and the other barnyard animals?

Chapters 6–10: Why and how do Abby and Ben reward Whittington?

Chapter 11: What do we learn about Ben in this chapter? Do you think Abby will be able to help him? Why or why not?

Chapters 12–15: What agreement is made with the rats? Do you think all the animals will keep their word? Why or why not?

Chapter 16: Why is it so hard for Ben to learn to read? Was learning to read hard for you or someone you know?

Chapters 17–22: Why is Dick's cat so valuable to the king? Will Dick regret leaving the cat behind?

Chapters 23–25: Why doesn't Ben want to go to a special class? What could his friends do to make it easier? What could you do to help someone who is having difficulty learning?

Chapters 26–29: Where does Dick see the cat again? How do you think they recognized each other?

Chapter 30: What does Ben observe in the Reading Recovery room? Do you think the teacher can really help him? Why or why not?

Chapters 31–33: What do we learn about Whittingham? How does this information help us understand his name?

Chapters 34–36: Do you think Dick will marry Mary? Why or why not?

Chapters 37–39: In what ways is Ben like Dick Whittingham?

Chapters 40–45: Why is being able to read so important to Ben? How does it make him feel?

Orthopedic Impairment

Big Mama by Tony Crunk (Margot Apple). 2000. Grade. K+

Billy Boyd's grandmother, Big Mama, turns everything into an adventure. She joins him and the neighborhood children, one of whom is in a wheelchair, in their fun and games.

- What does Big Mama use to make a space capsule?
- Why does Big Mama make the children mow Mrs. Todd's yard for the rest of the summer?
- What do the children see walking to and from Woody's?
- Who do you think is in the wheelchair? Who pushes him and helps this person walk?

Chuck Close Up Close by Jan Greenberg and Sandra Jordan. 1998. Grade 3+

This is a biography of Chuck Close, a revisionist artist with a learning disability who later in life has a spinal artery collapse, which leads to paralysis. After months of rehabilitation, he develops a way to continue his painting.

Chapter 1: Why is school hard for Chuck? How does he study?

Chapter 2: What does Chuck mean when he says, "I wanted the viewer to get lost in the painting"?

Chapter 3: Who does Chuck paint? Why?

Chapter 4: What is Big Joe? How does it work?

Chapter 5: What is "the event"? How does it affect Chuck?

Cruise Control by Terry Trueman. 2004. Grade 7+

Paul, a high school senior and gifted athlete, struggles with many things in his life, including his disrespect for his father; the love and shame he feels for his younger brother, Shawn, who has cerebral palsy; and his own violent outbursts. This is a companion book to *Stuck in Neutral*, told from Shawn's brother's point of view.

Chapters 1–3: Why is it ironic that Paul sometimes envies Shawn? Would you? Do you agree that it's hard to love someone who can't love back?

Chapters 4–6: How are Eddie and Paul alike and different? Why do you think Paul acts "slow?" Why won't Paul acknowledge Shawn in any way?

Chapters 7–9: Why does Paul feel embarrassed to feel embarrassed? Would you feel the same way? What do you think is the point of Shawn's life?

Chapters 10–12: Do you think Cindy's suspicions about her dad are justified? Why or why not? What do you think Shawn and his dad did while they were alone for two hours?

Chapters 13–15: Why does Paul feel he can't leave his family? Why do you think Paul got so wasted and drove drunk when he knew it was wrong?

Chapters 16–18: How well do you think Paul's team will do in the state tournament? Why is it ironic that Tim, rather than Paul, is in jail?

Chapters 19–20: How has Paul changed? What changed him?

Chapters 21–23: What does Paul mean by "maybe deserves doesn't have much to do with it"? Why does Paul think the game doesn't matter in the same way that so many bigger things matter?

Disabilities by Mutiya Vision (Ignacio Alcantara). 2004. Grade K+

A young boy born without arms learns to appreciate and love himself for who he is and who he can become.

- How does the young boy make up for not having arms? How does he write, paint, and eat?

- What do you think happened to make him no longer feel ashamed?

- How do some people treat the young boy? Would you want to be his friend?

- What does the young boy do when other people tease or feel sorry for him?

- He says beauty isn't just how you look. Is he right? Why or why not?

Harry and Willy and Carrothead by Judith Caseley. 1991. Grade K+

Despite a prosthetic left hand, Harry's abilities are similar to those of other children. At school, Harry dispels myths about his disability and helps two classmates separated by their differences to become friends.

- How is Harry different from other children? How is he like other children?

- What is a prosthesis?

- How does Oscar feel about being called "Carrothead"?

- What are some of Harry's strengths?

- What lesson did Harry teach Willy about friendship?

Harry Sue by Sue Stauffacher. 2005. Grade 4+

Harry Sue already has several strikes against her at age eleven. Both of her parents are convicted felons; she lives with her abusive Granny, who "has no heart"; and her best friend, Homer, has quadriplegia and won't come out of his treehouse. Harry Sue compares her life and others around her to the characters and events in *The Wizard of Oz*—the real story from the book by L. Frank Baum, not the contrived movie version.

Chapters 1–4: Why does Harry Sue's mother choose that name for her? What is the story behind your name?

Chapters 5–7: How does Homer become injured? Who do you think is suffering most because of his accident?

Chapters 8–9: What is ironic about the different outcomes of Harry Sue's and Homer's falls?

Chapters 10–12: Why does Harry Sue's mother think authors are the mysterious ones? Do you agree?

Chapters 13–15: If you were Homer, would you find it difficult to be motivated? Why or why not?

Chapters 16–18: Why is Granny so prejudiced against Mr. Olatanju? Why doesn't Harry Sue feel the same way? What did Harry Sue learn from Mr. Olatanju?

Chapters 19–21: Why does Harry Sue think the long road ahead of her isn't made of yellow bricks? Do you agree? How would you describe the road ahead of your life?

Chapters 22–23: Why does Harry Sue think Homer's "real life" was over? Do you agree?

Chapters 24–27: What does J-Cat show Homer? Do you think it will motivate him?

Chapters 28–31: How is sickness of the heart worse than physical pain?

Chapters 32–37: What does the phrase "some things require the dark night to bloom" mean to you?

Knockin' on Wood by Lynne Barasch (Lynne Barasch). 2004. Grade K+

As a young boy Clayton loved to dance, but at age twelve his left leg got caught in a machine and had to be amputated. No one thought Clayton would walk again, let alone become a professional dancer.

- Why do you think Clayton's mother didn't want him to dance when he was young?
- How does Clayton lose his leg?
- What does his uncle make for Clayton?
- Why do they call him Peg Leg Bates?
- Where does he perform?

Mama Zooms by Jane Cowen-Fletcher (Jane Cowen-Fletcher). 1993. Grade K+

A young boy describes his mama's "zooming machine" as he rides on her lap and pretends she is his racehorse, ship, car, airplane, train, buckboard wagon, wave, and spaceship. The boy has fanciful experiences and sees no limitations in his mother, who uses a wheelchair.

- What do you think the owner of the hats on the rack likes to do?
- What do you think a "zooming machine" is?
- Would you like to "zoom" with your mom like this boy?
- Do you know anyone who uses a wheelchair? How does the wheelchair help that person go places? How could this person get around if he or she didn't have a wheelchair?

Nathan's Wish: A Story About Cerebral Palsy by Laurie Lears (Stacey Shuett). 2005. Grade K+

Nathan, a young boy with cerebral palsy, wishes he could walk by himself so he could help Miss Sandy, a raptor rehabilitator, with her chores. He becomes inspired when Fire, a screech owl that cannot fly, finds another purpose in life.

- What does Nathan use to help him move around?
- Why does Nathan name the screech owl Fire?
- What does Nathan learn from Fire?
- How does Nathan help Miss Sandy?
- What can you learn from Nathan?

Private School by Avi (Bill Farnsworth). 2001. Grade 3+

Noah lives with his parents on a farm in the 1880s. Because there are no schools nearby, Aunt Dora comes to teach him. The family is surprised to see her arrive in a wheelchair, the result of an accident that partially paralyzed her. Noah isn't convinced that reading will do him any good on the prairie until Aunt Dora shows him how.

Chapter 1: What are Noah's chores? How are they alike or different from your chores? Why doesn't Noah just go to school?

Chapter 2: How does Aunt Dora arrive? Why does she need to use a wheelchair? Do you think it will be difficult for Aunt Dora to get around the prairie?

Chapter 3: Why doesn't Noah want to learn? Do you ever feel this way? When and what happened?

Chapters 4–5: How does Aunt Dora convince Noah that learning to read can help him on the prairie? How do you think Aunt Dora felt being pushed on the bumpy ground?

Chapters 6–7: What is a primer? How has Noah's life changed?

Chapter 8: What constellation does Noah find in the night sky? Find your own constellation and name it. In what ways will Noah now be his best teacher?

Seal Surfer by Michael Foreman (Michael Foreman). 1997. Grade K+

After seeing a young seal born and then grow throughout the seasons, Ben develops a special bond with the animal. Although not addressed in the text, Ben is seen in a wheelchair and using crutches.

- Can you find a chair in the first picture? What kind of chair is it? Why is it there?

- What is lying next to Ben in the second picture? How do they work?

- With whom does Ben surf? Why is the surfboard connected to his hand?

- Why is Ben's grandfather missing at the end of the story?

- What colors does the artist use to illustrate the ocean?

Small Steps by Louis Sachar. 2006. Grade 5+

Armpit, having been released from juvenile detention camp, is convinced by fellow detainee X-Ray to earn extra money by scalping concert tickets. Armpit ends up taking his friend, ten-year-old Ginny who has cerebral palsy, to the concert. They meet the famous teenage diva, Kaira, with whom Armpit becomes romantically involved.

Chapters 1–3: How does Armpit help Ginny? How does Ginny help Armpit?

Chapters 4–6: Why do you think Ginny gives each of her stuffed animals a disability?

Chapters 7–9: Why do people think Ginny "is retarded"? Will Armpit regret getting involved with X-Ray's scheme?

Chapters 10–12: Which stuffed animal would you vote for? Why?

Chapters 13–15: Why do you think Tatiana really can't go to the concert with Armpit? Why do the police think Ginny is on drugs?

Chapters 16–18: How would you feel if you'd gotten special treatment at a rock concert?

Chapters 19–21: Why do you think Armpit tells Kaira he only takes small steps? What does that mean? Why does Armpit lie to the detective? What would you have done?

Chapters 22–25: Does Kaira really regret sending Armpit the letter? Have you ever done something you regretted?

Chapters 26–29: What does the story about the donkey standing halfway between two haystacks have anything to do with Armpit's life?

Chapters 30–32: On his trip, Armpit only thinks about one person back home—Ginny. Why?

Chapters 33–36: Will Armpit successfully complete his small steps? Why or why not? Will he ever see Kaira again?

Stuck in Neutral by Terry Trueman. 2000. Grade 7+

Fourteen-year-old Shawn McDaniel is happy to be alive despite being trapped inside his body with no muscle control due to cerebral palsy. No one knows his thoughts or even that he has any. His father views Shawn's life as endless torment, and Shawn is afraid his father may be planning to kill him. This is a companion book to *Cruise Control,* told from Shawn's point of view

Chapters 1–2: Shawn describes his life as "good news–bad news." What would your good news–bad news be about yourself? How did Shawn learn to read?

Chapters 3–4: What does Shawn mean by "in ways Dad is nothing like he appears to be on all those TV talk shows, and in other ways he's exactly like he seems on them"?

Chapters 5–6: Why does Shawn think his Dad may want to kill him? What does Shawn experience when he's having a seizure? Why does he refer to them as miracles?

Chapters 7–8: Why does Shawn compare his classroom to a zoo? Do you agree? Why or why not?

Chapters 9–10: How would it feel to know no one around you could really understand who you are and what you are capable of becoming?

Chapters 11–12: Do you think Earl Detraux deserves to be punished? Why or why not? In your opinion, why does Paul defend his brother so violently?

Chapters 13–16: Why can't Shawn get death off his mind? What do you think happens after the book ends?

Susan Laughs by Jeanne Willis (Tony Ross). 2000. Grade K+

Susan feels the same as other children, and she does the same things that they do. The reader doesn't learn until the end of the story that Susan is in a wheelchair.

- Can you do all the things Susan does?

- When do you feel happy, sad, angry, or proud like Susan?

- How is Susan different from you?

- Would you like to be Susan's friend? Why?

The View from Saturday by E. L. Konigsburg. 1996. Grade 4+, Newbery Medal Book
Mrs. Olinski, returning to teaching ten years after being paralyzed in a car accident, selects a group of four brilliant, but unlikely, teammates to be her sixth-grade Academic Bowl Team.

Chapter 1: Why do you think Mrs. Olinski chooses Noah first for the Academic Bowl Team?

Chapter 2: What defines multiculturalism and diversity? Does Mrs. Olinski meet the criteria for being diverse? Why or why not?

Chapter 3: What awakens in Ethan through the course of this chapter? How much can be attributed to Julian?

Chapter 4: If you were Julian, what would you have done? Do you think Mrs. Olinski knows about "The Souls"? Why or why not?

Chapter 5: Why does Mrs. Olinski decide not to choose Ham, but Julian instead?

Chapter 6: What is meant by the statement, "Mrs. Sharkey said they gave new meaning to the term 'bottoms up'"?

Chapter 7: How do The Souls and sixth graders celebrate? In what way was it unusual? How would you have celebrated?

Chapters 8–9: How do you think Mr. Singh knew about Mrs. Olinski's decision not to select Ham, but Julian instead?

Chapters 10–12: Explain why Mrs. Olinski chooses the members of the Academic Bowl. Why does she feel something is missing? Have you ever felt that way? When?

The Westing Game by Ellen Raskin. 1978. Grade 4+, Newbery Medal Book
The tenants of a new condominium building, including Chris who uses a wheelchair, learn that they may be heirs to the estate of Sam Westing. His will states that his murderer is among the heirs. In teams of two, they must use clues to identify the murderer, with the winning team inheriting the Westing fortune.

Chapters 1–2: What might we conclude about Chris from what we know of him so far?

Chapters 3–7: Why was Theo offended by Flora's reaction to Chris's convulsions? How does Grace Wexler's attitude toward the other heirs reflect several stereotypes common to our society?

Chapters 8–9: How is Chris's decision to wait for his smarter partner ironic? In what ways might Chris be considered smarter?

Chapters 10–12: Like Sydelle and Turtle, many people have "crutches" that they hide behind to avoid revealing their true selves. What are some common crutches among people you know?

Chapters 13–14: Why does Chris feel that he and Sydelle are "really friends," as opposed to his relationships with the others? Why does Chris decide not to sign the check?

Chapters 15–17: Why would it be beneficial for the other heirs to talk to Chris? Why did Angela bomb herself? Do you think she was right or wrong about "what really counts"?

Chapter 18: How does Flora's reference to her daughter as "exceptional" reveal a perspective different from the harsher terms "retarded" and "Mongoloid" that Sandy uses? How are the characters changing in this chapter?

Chapters 19–30: How do Grace Wexler's, James Shin Hoo's, and Judge J. J. Ford's attitudes change by the end of this book?

The Wheel on the School by Meindert DeJong. 1954. Grade 4+, Newbery Medal Book
    Schoolgirl Lina realizes that there are no storks in her town of Shora. Her teacher decides that Lina and her five schoolmates will spend time locating a wheel to place on top of the school so the storks can nest. The story follows the students' quest to find a wheel and how the whole town, especially old Janus, a man who has lost his legs, helps to secure a wheel so that storks can begin their nesting season in Shora.

    Chapters 1–2: What does the town of Shora look like? How does it compare with your hometown? Do you know anyone like Grandmother Sibble III? If so, describe him or her.

    Chapters 3–4: Why don't storks come to Shora? How do the children and teacher plan on getting storks to their town?

    Chapters 5–6: Who is Janus? Why is he in a wheelchair? Do you know anyone in a wheelchair? If so, describe him or her.

    Chapters 7–8: How does Auka solve both the tin man and Evert's problems? Do you think all the trouble Lina has is worth the wheel that she finds? Why or why not?

    Chapters 9–10: In what ways is Janus the hero? Do you think the others are surprised at what he's able to do? Why or why not?

    Chapters 11–12: Why do you think Janus suddenly decides to attend church?

    Chapters 13–14: Why are the children so confident that Janus knows more about storks than the newspaper? Who are the first to see storks after the storm? Why are they the first to see them?

    Chapter 15: What circumstances allow the children actually to hold storks? Do you think storks will return next year?

Wintering Well by Lea Wait. 2004. Grade 4+
    Will's plans for a career in farming are ruined after his leg is amputated. He and his sister, Cassie, go to stay with their sister in town and learn that there are more opportunities available to them than farm life. This story is set in the early 1800s.

    Chapters 1–3: Do you think Will's accident was Cassie's fault? What superstitions does Ma try to help Will?

    Chapters 4–6: How does Will's surgery differ from how it would be done today? Why does Will wish he had died? Would you feel the same way?

    Chapters 7–9: How do Will and Reverend Adams perceive Will's accident differently?

    Chapters 10–12: Why doesn't Will go to school? Why were the two boys so rude to Will? What would you have done if you were one of them?

    Chapters 13–16: How has Will changed according to Cassie? How has the role of women changed since the time of this story?

    Chapters 17–19: Why isn't Will's leg of pine shaped like a real leg? In your opinion, what profession will he choose to pursue? Why?

    Chapters 20–22: How does learning to be a doctor differ today from the process described in the story?

Chapters 23–25: Why don't mariners learn to swim? Do you think this is smart?

Chapters 26–28: Why could Dr. Theobold save Will but not his own wife? Where does Dr. Theobold take Will? What do they do? Why is Cassie so curious about Will's visit?

Chapters 29–31: Do you think Davey and Thom will continue to bully Will? How have Will and Cassie changed since the beginning of the story?

Traumatic Brain Injury

Bringing Nettie Back by Nancy Hope Wilson. 1992. Grade 4+
Eleven-year-old Clara invites twin sisters, Patty and Nettie, to her grandmother's farm for the summer. Clara and Patty become best friends, but during the school year, Nettie has a stroke, leaving her with a serious brain injury. After being in a coma for months, Nettie slowly recovers but will never be the lively, witty person she was before. Patty and Clara learn to accept Nettie as the person she has become.

Chapters 1–6: Why did Nettie always want to go to Clara's house? Why was it important to Clara to have the dinner table set perfectly?

Chapters 7–9: How does Clara's father make her feel? How does Clara's mom describe what happened to Nettie when she becomes ill?

Chapters 10–11: How does Nettie's drawing of Clara make Clara feel? What is a shunt? How is Nettie different when she comes home from the hospital?

Chapters 12–13: Why doesn't Nettie draw anymore? Do you think she will ever draw again?

Chapters 14–15: Why does Clara stop playing her banjo? What does Clara learn about her father at the end of the book? What does Clara believe will "bring Nettie back"? Does it work? Why or why not?

Visual Impairment and Blindness

By the Shores of Silver Lake by Laura Ingalls Wilder. 1939. Grade 4+, Newbery Honor Book
The Ingalls family spends the winter isolated in the Dakota Territory while preparing to build a homestead in the spring. Mary has gone blind from scarlet fever and Laura "sees" for her by describing all their surroundings. *Note: The chapters in this book are not numbered. For convenience, we list the questions and corresponding chapters in their numerical order.*

Chapters 1–3: How does Mary become blind? How can she "see" the red velvet of the seats on the train?

Chapters 4–6: What does Laura think is the most wonderful thing, and what does she secretly wish Pa could do? Have you ever felt this way? When?

Chapters 7–10: What does Mary say about how Laura describes things? What can Mary sew without seeing? What does Pa say about covered wagons in the future? Is he correct?

Chapters 11–12: Why are the men so upset about their paychecks? Why does it work this way? What does Laura think about teaching?

Chapters 13–15: Describe the Ingalls's winter home? What do they do during the evening for entertainment? What would you do?

Chapters 16–17: How does Mary "see" when she sews? Do you think this would be hard? Why or why not?

Chapters 18–20: What kinds of gifts do the family make for each other? What would you make for your family members? Why do you think Mary hears people outside before anyone else does?

Chapters 21–23: Why is Laura so excited by what Mrs. Boast brought? What does Reverend Alden know that could help Mary?

Chapters 24–26: How does the Ingalls family earn money? For what does Laura hope her parents can save their money? Why do you think she feels this way?

Chapters 27–29: What happens to the Ingalls' their first night in town? What is moving like for them?

Chapters 30–32: What is the significance of Chapter 30's title? How do they take care of the mosquitoes? How does this compare with what we do today?

 The Double-Digit Club by Marion Dane Bauer. 2004. Grade 3+

Sarah feels abandoned when her best friend, Paige, joins a clique of other girls. Sarah finds some solace in visiting her elderly neighbor, who is blind, until she makes some bad decisions trying to win Paige back.

Chapters 1–2: What is the double-digit club, and who is eligible to join? Why do you think Paige decided to join?

Chapters 3–4: How do you think Miss Berglund matches her clothes and knows when to stop pouring lemonade? What is the gathering eye bouquet game?

Chapters 5–6: Why is Sarah so interested in the doll? Does Sarah do the right thing?

Chapters 7–8: What does Miss Berglund mean when she says people should appreciate what they have when they have it?

Chapters 9–10: Who decided to leave the DDC and why? Why do you think Paige was in Miss Berglund's house?

Chapter 11: How are Sarah and Paige taking advantage of Miss Berglund's blindness?

Chapters 12–13: How are Sarah and Paige different from one another? How are they alike? Are you more like Sarah or Paige? Why?

Chapters 14–15: How can hatred and love be all mixed together? Why do you think Miss B. wasn't upset at Sarah? Do you think Sarah and Paige will start their own club?

From Charlie's Point of View by Richard Scrimger. 2005. Grade 7+

Seventh graders Bernadette and Charlie, who has a visual impairment, have been best friends for years. When Charlie's father is accused of stealing money from bank machines, Bernadette, Charlie, and a third friend, Lewis, decide to solve the case by discovering the real Stocking Bandit.

Chapter 1: How does Bernadette help Charlie? How does Charlie help Bernadette? What is a Louis Light? How does it work? What is O and M? How does Charlie feel about Mrs. Vox's announcement? How would you feel? Who do you think is the real Stocking Bandit? Why?

Chapter 2: Decribe Charlie, Bernadette, Lewis, and Frank. What do they have in common? How are they different? What would you write about if asked what you *didn't* do last summer?

Chapter 3: What would you have done if you'd seen Frank choking? Why do you think Mrs. Yodelschmidt goes out in the rain? How does Lewis's mother embarrass him? How would you feel?

Chapter 4: How do the other students react to Charlie in the lunchroom? Why? How would you feel if you were Charlie? Would you have gone inside the vault like Charlie does? Why or why not?

Chapter 5: Why is the Stocking Bandit's choice of the Pater vault ironic? How does time change throughout the story? Who do you think Gideon really is? What is the symbolism of music that surrounds his presence?

Gentle's Holler by Kerry Madden. 2005. Grade 5+

Set in the 1960s, twelve-year-old Livy Two spends most of her time doing chores and caring for her siblings in the hills of North Carolina. Tragedy seems to rest on the family including Daddy's difficulty finding work and learning that three-year-old Gentle is blind.

Chapters 1–2: What are some of Livy Two's favorite books? What are your favorite books? Why is Livy Two worried about Gentle? Do you think her worries are justified?

Chapters 3–5: Where are some of Livy Two's secret places? Do you have any secret places?

Chapters 6–8: How does Louise describe colors to Gentle? How would you describe colors? What does Livy Two mean when she says she already feels like she's got invisible ropes tied to her? Have you ever felt that way? When?

Chapters 9–11: Could Uncle Hazard become a seeing eye dog? Why or why not? What does Livy Two and her parents learn about Gentle? How did it happen?

Chapters 12–14: What is Miss Attickson going to suggest that all lending libraries carry? Does your school or public library carry such things?

Chapters 15–17: Why do you think Grandma Horace cares about Uncle Hazard? How is Grandma Horace changing in Livy Two's eyes?

Chapters 18–20: Do you think Daddy will be OK? Will he ever come home?

📖 **The Great Gilly Hopkins** by Katherine Paterson. 1978. Grade 4+, Newbery Honor Book

Eleven-year-old Gilly, a foster child, changes to another home with desires to locate her real mother. When faced with that opportunity, however, she changes her mind. She learns to love and respect her new foster family and Mr. Randolph, an old black neighbor who is blind. *Note: The chapters in this book are not numbered. For convenience, we list the questions and corresponding chapters in their numerical order.*

Chapters 1–2: What have you learned about Gilly at this point in the story? Why does Gilly run away when she sees Mr. Randolph? What would you have done?

Chapters 3–4: Why do you think Gilly started the fight at school? Is she right in taking the money? Why or why not?

Chapters 5–6: Why is Gilly so mean to Agnes? How is the relationship between Gilly and Trotter beginning to change?

Chapters 7–8: How are Gilly and Miss Harris alike? How are they different? Do you think they are a good match for one another? Why or why not?

Chapters 9–10: When do you think Gilly will see her mother again?

Chapters 11–12: Why has Gilly changed her mind about leaving Trotter's home? How would you feel if you were Gilly?

Chapters 13–14: Will Gilly ever see Trotter, W. E., or Mr. Randolph again? Do you think she'll be happy in her new home? Why or why not?

Chapters 15–16: Why do you think the author used letters to tell the story? Why is Gilly disappointed at the airport? Do you think she will live happily ever after? Why or why not?

📖 **The Hickory Chair** by Lisa Rowe Fraustino (Benny Andrews). 2001. Grade K+

When Louis's Gran dies, she leaves to each of her favorite people a note hidden in one of her favorite things that they are to keep. Louis, although he is blind, finds several of the notes, but no one finds his—until he's as old as Gran was when she hid the notes.

• Would it be hard to play hide-and-seek if you were blind? How does Louis do it?

• Why does Gran leave hidden notes all over the house?

• Why can't they find Louis's note? What do you think Gran would want him to have?

• When does Louis finally find the note?

Knots on a Counting Rope by Bill Martin, Jr., and John Archambault (Ted Rand). 1987. Grade K+

A Native American grandfather and his blind grandson reminisce about the boy's turbulent birth, how he learned to ride a horse, and how he participated in a memorable horse race. The grandfather urges the boy to learn his own story by heart.

- How did Boy-Strength-of-Blue-Horses learn to ride a horse?
- How was he able to see? How could he know which way to turn?
- Are blind people more the same or more different from other people?
- Why is grandfather proud even though Boy-Strength-of-Blue-Horses does not win the race?
- Why is it important for Boy-Strength-of-Blue-Horses to tell the story on his own?

Melanie by Carol Carrick (Alisher Dianov). 1996. Grade K+

Melanie's grandfather goes in search of someone to heal her blindness. When he doesn't return, Melanie searches for him and rescues him—and many others—from the spell of a troll.

- What is Grandfather searching for?
- How does Melanie know which way to walk?
- Do you think Melanie looks like she has blindness? Why or why not?
- Whom does Melanie save? How does she do it?
- Why is Melanie happy even though she is not cured of her blindness?

Ray Charles by Sharon Bell Mathis (George Ford). 2001. Grade K+

Ray Charles, a black child born to a poor family and who is blinded at a young age, grows up to be a famous musician.

- Have you heard of Ray Charles?
- Why didn't Ray's mother baby him?
- How would you feel if you'd been tricked in the race like Ray is tricked?
- How does Ray read and write music? How does he play chess and cards and tell time?
- What has happened to Ray since this book was written?

Sarah's Sleepover by Bobbie Rodriguez (Mark Graham). 2000. Grade K+

When Sarah's cousins arrive for a sleepover and the lights go off, Sarah, who is blind, shows them how to get around in the dark.

- Why do you think Sarah can hear cars coming before anyone else?
- Why don't the girls play checkers or musical chairs? What do they end up playing?
- Why isn't Sarah scared when the lights go out? Would you have been scared?
- How does Sarah help the other girls not be scared?
- Why does Sarah think this is the best sleepover weekend ever?

See the Ocean by Estelle Condra (Linda Crockett-Blassingame). 1994. Grade K+

Each year Nellie and her family spend time at their beach house. As they are driving to the beach, her brother tries to be the first to see the ocean. One year a thick mist covered the valleys, and no one could "see" the ocean, except Nellie, who is blind.

- Why do you think Nellie loves the ocean?

- What do Nellie and her brother do on the beach?

- Why does Nellie ask so many questions about the ocean?

- How does Nellie describe the ocean?

- Why could Nellie "see" the ocean when no one else could?

Sing to the Stars by Mary Brigid Barrett (Sandra Speidel). 1994. Grade K+

Mr. Washington, who lost his sight after a car accident, is always able to recognize the rhythm of Ephram's steps on the street. Mr. Washington, a great classical pianist, invites Ephram, who takes violin lessons, to play at the neighborhood fundraiser concert after noticing Ephram's talent in music. They then perform together at the concert by playing "Amazing Grace" in the dark.

- How does Mr. Washington recognize Ephram's steps?

- How did Mr. Washington lose his sight?

- What does Ephram learn about Mr. Washington's talents from the conversation with his grandmother?

- Why do you think Mr. Washington stopped playing piano after the car accident?

- How does Mr. Washington "see" in the dark?

These Happy Golden Years by Laura Ingalls. 1943. Grade 6+, Newbery Honor Book

Fifteen-year-old Laura Ingalls begins teaching twelve miles from home, living in unhappy circumstances. Every weekend she gets to go home, being driven through the snow by Almanzo Wilder. After moving home, Laura gives her money to her parents to help pay for Mary's education at the college for blind students. Laura enjoys her time with Almanzo. *Note: The chapters in this book are not numbered. For convenience, we list the questions and corresponding chapters in their numerical order.*

Chapters 1–4: Where does Mary attend school? Are there similar schools in your community?

Chapters 5–12: What does Laura do with her money? How can she make more money now than she could before? If you were Laura, how would you spend the money?

Chapters 13–15: What has Mary learned at college?

Chapters 16–17: What do Laura and Mary talk about on their walks?

Chapters 18–20: How does the family feel about what Mary writes in her letter?

Chapters 21–33: What do Mary and Laura say about growing up? Do you agree? Why or why not?

Things Not Seen by Andrew Clements. 2002. Grade 6+

Fifteen-year-old Bobby wakes up one morning and finds he is invisible. He meets and befriends Andrea, a girl who is blind. Together and with help from their parents, they spend the next month trying to determine what caused his condition and how to reverse it.

Chapters 1–3: How are Bobby and a Stealth Bomber alike? What clues does the author provide that the girl is blind?

Chapters 4–6: What are the new rules?

Chapters 7–8: What does Bobby mean when he tells the reader that fear keeps feeding itself and then it gets you to feed it? Have you ever felt that way?

Chapters 9–11: Describe what Bobby observes about the eighteen-year-old. Why do you think it's so easy for Bobby to talk to the blind girl?

Chapters 12–14: What are the parallels between Bobby's and Alicia's lives? How does Bobby stereotype the girls in his school?

Chapters 15–16: Do you think Bobby should be classified as having a disability? Why or why not?

Chapters 17–19: How is Alicia good for Bobby? How is Bobby good for Alicia?

Chapters 20–22: Why is it ironic that Bobby can look at everything and be bored, while Alicia has "nothing but her own thoughts" and does not get bored?

Chapters 23–25: How do Bobby's and Sheila's reactions to their condition differ? How exactly do Bobby and Alicia communicate through the internet?

Chapters 26–29: Would you have chosen what Bobby chooses or what Sheila chooses? Why? Will Bobby and Alicia's relationship last? Why or why not?

III. Lesson Plans

Picture Books

Lesson 1: *Harry and Willy and Carrothead* (Orthopedic Impairment)

Lesson 2: *Hooway for Wodney Wat* (Communication Disorder)

Lesson 3: *Ian's Walk* (Autism)

Lesson 4: *Knots on a Counting Rope* (Visual Impairment)

Lesson 5: *Thank You, Mr. Falker* (Learning Disability)

Lesson Plan 1

Book: *Harry and Willy and Carrothead* by Judith Caseley (Judith Caseley, illustrator). 1991. Grade K+	
Global Purpose: Recognize strengths of people with disabilities.	
Objective: After reading the book, students will list three strengths of the main character, Harry, as well as three of their own strengths.	
Materials: pencils, paper	
Pre-Reading Activities	• Read the title of the book, show the cover, and ask, "Which boy do you think Harry is? Willy? Carrothead? Why?" • "Do you think the name 'Carrothead' is a nice term? Why or why not?" • "Do you notice anything special or different about any of these boys?" (Harry is wearing a prosthesis.) "Why do you think his arm looks different from yours or mine?"
During Reading Activities	• After reading the first page, ask, "Now, who knows why his arm and hand on the cover of the book look different?" • "What do you think Harry will be able to do without a hand like yours? Let's read the story and find out."
Post-Reading Activities	• "Do you think Harry is a 'poor little thing'? Why or why not?" • "What was Harry able to do even though he didn't have a hand?" (run, climb, finger paint) • "What is a prosthesis?" • "What was Harry able to do after he got his prosthesis?" (eat, make crafts, throw paper airplanes, throw balls, paint fingernails) • "How was Harry a good friend to Oscar? Could you be brave enough to stop someone from calling your friend a bad name?"
Closure	• Have the students write or draw three of Harry's strengths, then three of their strengths.

Lesson Plan 2

Book: *Hooway for Wodney Wat* by Helen Lester (Lynn Munsinger, illustrator). 1999. Grade 1+	
Global Purpose: To defend oneself or others when bullied.	
Objective: After the teacher reads the book to the students, they will use puppets to role-play different bullying situations.	
Materials: puppets, classroom theater stage (if available), picture of a capybara and a rat	
Pre-Reading Activities	• Show a picture of a South American capybara. Explain that a capybara is the largest living rodent (it can be up to 4 feet long and weigh 145 pounds). • Compare the capybara with a common rat. Show a picture of a common rat (usually up to 9 inches long and can weigh up to 300 grams).
During Reading Activities	While reading the book, stop periodically to ask these questions: • "How do you think Rodney feels about not being able to pronounce his r's?" • "Why doesn't Rodney just ignore the rodents when they tease him about his speech?" • "Do you think everyone in the class was afraid of Camilla Capybara? Why or why not?" • "When did Rodney start to feel confident?" • "How did Rodney's speech problems help the other rodents accept him?"
Post-Reading Activities	• Have students reenact the story using puppets. • Have small groups of students develop and perform a short puppet show about (1) standing up to bullies or (2) accepting students who are different.
Closure	• Discuss real situations in which the students have been bullied and how they stood up to the bullies. • Discuss real situations in which the students have accepted someone who was different from them. • Have students make a plan to stop bullying the next time they see it.

Lesson Plan 3

Book: *Ian's Walk* by Laurie Lears (Karen Ritz, illustrator). 1998. Grade K+	
Global Purpose: To increase students' knowledge of and sensitivity to people with sensory disabilities.	
Objective: After hearing the story read, students will create a collage about their sensory likes and dislikes.	
Materials: Large piece of butcher paper, crayons, markers, magazines, paint, crayons, stencils, scissors, "Our Five Senses" worksheet	

Pre-Reading Activities	• Ask the students if they like the smell of bricks. Pass around a brick and have the students describe the smell. • State: "Today we are going to read a story about a child named Ian who likes to do things that may be a little different than what you and I like to do." • Show the cover of the book and read the title and author. • Ask the students what they think *Ian's Walk* is about.
During Reading Activities	• Stop periodically to ask questions about each of Ian's sensory experiences. • Ask students how Julie felt at the beginning compared with the end of the book. Why did Julie's reaction change?
Post-Reading Activities	• Tell the students that they are going to accompany Ian on his walk. • Pass out the worksheet "Our Five Senses" and give instructions as listed. Pass out art materials and assign students to six groups. • Retell the story rereading a few preselected passages for each specific group about what they should draw (1) Ian's home, (2) Nan's diner, (3) Mrs. Potter's flower stand, (4) post office bricks, (5) the pond, and (6) the bell. • Ask the class to draw the points along Ian's walk from his house to the bell in the park emphasizing what Ian liked at each point. • Have each group describe what they drew. • Have each group tell about their trip to the park and how they enjoy different sensory experiences than Ian enjoys. • Then have the students describe their trip from the park back to Ian's home, highlighting how they enjoy some of the same sensory experiences that Ian enjoys.
Closure	• Have the students identify which activities on their walk relate to each of the five senses. • Encourage the students to be more fully aware of their senses throughout the day.

Our Five Senses
Ian's Walk

Objective:

While in cooperative learning groups, the students will create an artistic depiction of what Ian perceives on his walk, using their creative reasoning, listening, writing, and artistic skills.

Directions:

- Listen to what Ian sees, hears, smells, feels, and tastes as the teacher reads *Ian's Walk*.

- You will be assigned to a group of students. Together you will focus on one part of the story: (1) Ian's home, (2) Nan's Diner, (3) Mrs. Potter's flower stand, (4) post office bricks, (5) the pond, or (6) the bell.

- As a group, discuss what Ian might have seen, heard, and felt at that part of the story.

- Use these ideas to create a collage or mural of Ian's walk with your group.

- Use any media (crayons, markers, magazines, paint, stencils, etc.) available.

From *Teaching About Disabilities Through Children's Literature* by Mary Anne Prater and Tina Taylor Dyches. Westport, CT: Teacher Ideas Press. Copyright © 2008.

Area: ☐ Ian's home ☐ Nan's diner ☐ Flower stand ☐ Post Office ☐ Pond ☐ Bell

Ian's Five Senses	Ideas
What does Ian see?	
What does Ian hear?	
What does Ian smell?	
What does Ian feel?	
What does Ian taste?	

Collage/Mural Ideas:

Lesson Plan 4

Book: *Knots on a Counting Rope* by Bill Martin, Jr., and John Archambault (Ted Rand, illustrator). 1987. Grade K+	
Global Purpose: Students will learn how individuals who are blind adapt by using their other senses.	
Objective: After reading the story and participating in the activities, students will verbally explain how they can "see" with their ears and hands.	
Materials: Paper bags with objects inside for each student, prerecorded tape or CD of sounds, tape recorder or CD player	
Pre-Reading Activities	• Ask, "What do you use your eyes, ears, hands to do?" "What would you do if you couldn't see, hear, or feel?" • Tell them you are going to read a story about a Navajo boy whose eyes did not work. He could not see like most people do.
During Reading Activities	• While reading, stop periodically to ask questions about the text and illustrations, such as, "Why is he, as a baby, reaching out to the horses if he can't see them?" "Why will he always have to live in the dark? What does that mean?" "Does he look like he's blind in the pictures?"
Post-Reading Activities	• Review the pages describing how the boy can see with his hands, ears, and skin. • Explain that they are going to experience seeing with their hands and ears just like the boy in the story. • Divide the class into three or four groups. Using a classroom helper for each group, students reach into a paper bag and, without looking, describe the object inside of it. Then have them pull out the items to "see" whether they are correct. • As a class discuss why they were able to "see" something with their hands. Ask, "What did the boy in the story see with his hands?" "What couldn't he feel?" "Why were some things easier to see with your hands?" • Explain that they are going to experience "seeing" with their ears. • Play a prerecorded tape or CD of everyday events (e.g., water running, phone ringing, airplane flying overhead, bell ringing, piano playing). Ask students what they "see" with their ears. Ask "What did the boy in the story see with his ears?" • Explain that people who cannot see with their eyes learn to see with other parts of their bodies like their hands and ears. • Ask students to explain how they could see with their ears and their hands.
Closure	• Review the objects that they *saw* with their eyes and hands. • Review what the boy could see with his hands and eyes and what he could not see.

Lesson Plan 5

Book: *Thank You, Mr. Falker* by Patricia Polacco (Patricia Polacco, illustrator). 1998. Grade K+	
Global Purpose: To increase students' awareness of and sensitivity to others' feelings.	
Objective: After hearing the story read, students will draw pictures representing the feelings of Trisha at various stages of the story.	
Materials: "Recognizing Feelings" worksheet, crayons, one honey candy for each student	
Pre-Reading Activities	• Give the students a small piece of honey candy. Ask if they like honey and why. Ask if they like reading books and why. • State: "Today we are going to read a story about a girl named Trisha who learns to love books and reading as much as she loves honey." • Show the cover of the book and ask students who they think Mr. Falker is and why someone wants to thank him.

During Reading Activities	• Stop periodically to highlight the pictures and ask questions about Tricia's feelings.
	• Ask students how Tricia felt when
	  – she was having trouble reading.
	  – Mr. Falker loved her drawings.
	  – Eric and the other children teased her.
	  – Mr. Falker helped her learn to read.

Post-Reading Activities	• Retell the story by focusing on the following situations:
	  Box 1: Trisha had trouble reading.
	  Box 2: Mr. Falker loved Trisha's drawing.
	  Box 3: Eric and the other children teased Trisha.
	  Box 4: Mr. Falker helped Trisha learn to read.
	• Pass out paper and crayons and the "Recognizing Feelings" worksheet. Ask students to draw a picture of how Trisha felt at those times.
	• Ask students to imagine themselves as students in Trisha's class and then to draw a picture on the back of their paper of how they would show they were her friend.
	• Ask students how they would feel if they were the little girl in the story and to share some times when they felt happy and when they felt sad.
	• Ask students to share a time when they helped someone who was being teased or how someone else helped them when they were being teased.

Closure	• Review how Mr. Falker helped Trisha and how they can help others who are being teased.

Recognizing Feelings
Thank You, Mr. Falker

Directions: Draw a picture of how Trisha felt at different times. On the back of this paper, draw a picture of how you could be Trisha's friend.

Trisha had trouble reading.	**Mr. Falker loved Trisha's drawing.**
Eric and the other children teased Trisha.	**Mr. Falker helped Trisha learn to read.**

IV. Unit Plans

Chapter Books

Unit 1: *The Bus People* (Multiple Disabilities)

Lesson 1: The Stigma of Disability

Lesson 2: Intellectual Disabilities: From *Slow* to *Go*!

Lesson 3: Communication Disorders: The Silent Ones

Lesson 4: Impact of Disabilities on Families

Unit 2: *Freak the Mighty* (Learning Disabilities and Orthopedic Impairment)

Lesson 1: Dispelling Stereotypes: The Unvanquished Truth

Lesson 2: To the Max: Success in the Face of Learning Disabilities

Lesson 3: Little Big Man: The Mighty Freak

Lesson 4: Real Life Heroes: Our Peers with Disabilities

Unit 3: *I Am an Artichoke* (Emotional and Behavioral Disorders)

Lesson 1: Defining Normal and Abnormal Behavior

Lesson 2: Understanding Persons with EBDs

Lesson 3: Understanding Eating Disorders

Lesson 4: Developing Friendships: What Should I Say?

Unit 4: *Joey Pigza Loses Control* (Attention-Deficit/Hyperactivity Disorder [ADHD])

Lesson 1: Characteristics of ADHD

Lesson 2: Attitudes Toward Disabilities

Lesson 3: Treatment of ADHD

Lesson 4: Read All About It!

Unit 5: *Tru Confessions* (Intellectual Disabilities)

Lesson 1: Etiology of Disabilities: The Mutant Shark Person

Lesson 2: Avoiding Victimization: "I Don't Want to Be Different"

Lesson 3: Accepting Differences: Just Who Has Special Needs?

Lesson 4: Growing Up: Spinning into Separate Futures

The Bus People: Unit 1, Lesson 1

The Stigma of Disability

Book: *The Bus People* by Rachel Anderson. 1989. Grade 7+	
Global Purpose: To understand and accept individuals with various severe disabilities.	
Objective: Students will discuss basic challenges, tendencies, needs, and strengths of persons with severe disabilities.	
Materials: *The Sneetches* by Dr. Seuss, Internet access for information about Down syndrome and autism, slips of paper, hat/box, cookies or other small treat for each student, student journals	
Pre-Reading Activities	• Read Dr. Seuss's book, *The Sneetches,* as a class. • Discuss why some Sneetches excluded and looked down on other Sneetches, emphasizing the absurdity of such behavior and reasoning. • Read Chapter 1 of *The Bus People* to the class. • Tell students that as they continue to read the book, some characters may remind them of the Sneetches.
During Reading Activities	• Ask students to begin reading Chapter 2 independently. While they are reading, conduct the "Trick or Treat?" activity following this lesson plan. • Find out what students know about Down syndrome and autism. • Have students continue to read Chapter 2 and then Chapter 4.

Post-Reading Activities	Divide the class into three groups, and assign one set of questions per group. Then discuss as a class the ideas shared in the groups.
	• Group 1: Rebecca's Challenges
	  – How does the wedding dress incident affect Rebecca?
	  – Why are rules important for Rebecca?
	  – Rebecca's family warns her that things will be different during and after the wedding. Why?
	• Group 2: Rebecca's Strengths
	  – How would you describe Rebecca's personality? What are her greatest strengths?
	  – How is Rebecca like those without disabilities?
	  – How does Rebecca overcome hurt feelings?
	• Group 3: Jonathan and Rebecca
	  – What stigmas affect Jonathan and Rebecca?
	  – How is Jonathan like those without disabilities?
	  – What makes the difference between how the story ended for Jonathan and how it ended for Rebecca?
	• Whole Class Discussion
	  – How might inclusion of students with disabilities in neighborhood schools foster positive attitudes toward persons with disabilities?

Closure	• Review main concepts from each chapter. • Ask, "Who are the Sneetches in these chapters?" • Have students write their feelings and thoughts about the chapters in their journal.

Trick or Treat? Activity

Preparation

Cut out slips of paper equal to the amount of students in your class today. On all but one of these, write the number 46. On the remaining slip, write the number 47. Fold the papers. Place them into a hat or box for a random drawing.

Activity

Tell students that while they are reading, you will be giving them a piece of paper. Ask them not to unfold the papers until you tell them to do so. Move around the room and **draw a slip of paper with a number for each student,** handing the paper to them one by one. After they have been disseminated, ask the students to show you their number privately. Present all students who received 46 with a cookie or other small treat, and the student who was given 47 with nothing. Say simply, "Sorry, wrong number."

Call the class to attention to discuss the criteria for receiving a cookie. Ask the students whether it was fair to withhold a cookie from the student who received 47, and discuss why or why not. (Be sure to give a cookie to the excluded student once this has been addressed.) This will lead into a discussion of Down syndrome. Explain that individuals with Down syndrome have 47 chromosomes instead of 46. (For information about Down syndrome, see http://www.ndsccenter.org/resources/package3.php; for information about autism, see http://www.autism-society.org/site/PageServer?pagename=about_ whatis_home.)

The Bus People: Unit 1, Lesson 2

Intellectual Disabilities: From *Slow* to *Go!*

Book: *The Bus People* by Rachel Anderson. 1989. Grade 7+	
Global Purpose: To understand and accept individuals with various severe disabilities.	
Objective: Students will discuss how appropriate instruction can help students with intellectual disabilities learn important life skills.	
Materials: "Life Skills" activity	
Pre-Reading Activities	• Divide the class into groups of four students. • Have each group complete the "Life Skills" activity worksheet. • Ask each group to share their answers with the class. • Explain that some special education programs focus on vital, everyday skills to increase individuals' quality of life. These programs are sometimes called "life skills."
During Reading Activities	• Read Chapter 7. • As a class, generate a list of what Danny can do by himself.
Post-Reading Activities	• Use the following questions to discuss Chapter 7: – What causes Danny's classmates to make fun of him? What could teachers and students have done to make Danny's experience in school more successful? – What do you like best about Danny? – Much of what Aunty Beth teaches Danny promotes self-sufficiency and the skills necessary to lead an enjoyable and successful life. How could a structured school environment effectively supplement Danny's productive home setting? – Can a life skills classroom in a regular school setting be even more effective than a "special school?" Why or why not? – How can we contribute to the success of our peers with special needs? What consequences will follow if they are not successful with their curriculum? • Invite a life skills special education teacher to speak about the types of skills students focus on in their class. Ask the teacher to bring samples of student progress in one or more areas.
Closure	• Discuss how the students can encourage their peers with disabilities to become more independent.

Life Skills Activity

Directions: Write down the skills you would need to accomplish each of the following:

Situation 1:

You want to invite a friend over for a party. What skills will you need to accomplish this?

Situation 2:

A shower pipe breaks and begins to flood the house. What skills will you need to fix the leak?

Situation 3:

A new movie has come out that you are very excited to see. What skills will you need to accomplish this?

Situation 4:

You have received a letter or e-mail message from a friend. You are interested in knowing what he or she has to say. What skills will you need in this situation?

Situation 5:

You have received your first paycheck. You want to save some money for your family's vacation, but you also have several bills to pay. What skills will enable you to succeed?

From *Teaching About Disabilities Through Children's Literature* by Mary Anne Prater and Tina Taylor Dyches. Westport, CT: Teacher Ideas Press. Copyright © 2008.

The Bus People: Unit 1, Lesson 3

Communication Disorders: The Silent Ones

Book: *The Bus People* by Rachel Anderson. 1989. Grade 7+	
Global Purpose: To understand and accept individuals with various severe disabilities.	
Objective: Students will express verbally and in writing their feelings and experiences relating to individuals with severe disabilities.	
Materials: "The Silent Ones" script, student journals	
Pre-Reading Activities	• Ask students to close their eyes. Read "The Silent Ones" script with excerpts from the stories of three *Bus People* characters with multiple disabilities, including communication disorders. • Ask: "Having heard these passages, what do you imagine these individuals to be like?" Discuss the students' responses.
During Reading Activities	• In pairs, have students read Chapter 5, stopping at "Rob's Story." • As a class read the section titled "Rob's Story." • Discuss the difference between Rob's and Ruby's attitudes and the attitudes of the other couples who came to visit Fleur. • Discuss Rob and Ruby's example. Ask: "How can we learn from their example? How can we emulate it? Should we associate with people with disabilities? Why or why not?"

Post-Reading Activities	• Ask students to write about their feelings in their journals on the following topics:
	
	  – What is your present feeling about people with disabilities?
	  – Have your feelings changed over time?
	  – Have you ever had experiences with persons with disabilities?
	  – What kind of relationship would you like to have with your peers with disabilities?
	
	• Have students share with the class some of their experiences with individuals with disabilities.

Closure	• Thank the students for sharing their thoughts and experiences. Encourage them to take the time to get to know their peers with disabilities better.

"The Silent Ones" Script

Directions: Close your eyes. Listen to the following passages, the thoughts of the silent ones, whose physical and emotional disabilities conceal the words they might otherwise speak.

"I live imprisoned inside a cage from which the only escape is a bus ride to school in the morning and a bus ride home in the evening" (pp. 22–23).

"When I am away at St. John's she will be able to go round the shops again, unencumbered. And while she shops, I will be learning skills. My slow mind will be taught to understand more quickly. My obstinate hands will be trained to obey, to whittle wood, to weave baskets. I will master the skill of dressing myself as other boys do, the skill of preparing my own medication.. . . . I will swallow down those tablets whole" (p. 34).

" 'Yeeerughaaah!' " I cried out. Transplant me a new body.. . . . Transplant me a voice so she can hear me cry from what I want. 'Yeeraghuuh' She puts her arms around me to re-enfold me in her suffocating embrace" (p. 37).

— —

"No one likes Marilyn. Gangling Marilyn's a fidget and a drip" (p. 50).

"Marilyn's feet are uneven, one sized 4 1/2 , the other sized 6, these mismatched feet attached to weak and wobbly ankles. Her eyes are not in alignment. She sees the world differently.. . . With her crooked eyes, she sees it sour and yellow" (pp. 50–51).

— —

"Once upon a time, there was a somebody named Fleur. Fleur did not like to talk. Fleur did not like to walk. Fleur did not like to run. Fleur did not like to think. Fleur always sat quietly . . . her eyes to the window. Fleur needed the light. Long ago . . . Fleur was in another place where it was dark" (pp. 53-54).

"Fleur could not always remember who she was, or why Fleur was. Fleur did not want to remember" (p. 54).

"Fleur . . . tried not to think of the small dark cupboard under the stairs. There were fleas in the cupboard. And rags. And smells. And fear. Fleur's mummy and Fleur's daddy were angry people who hauled Fleur by the arm to the cupboard beside the fireplace and made Fleur crawl inside and then the door was closed . . . and Fleur was alone in the dark" (pp. 55–56).

From *Teaching About Disabilities Through Children's Literature* by Mary Anne Prater and Tina Taylor Dyches. Westport, CT: Teacher Ideas Press. Copyright © 2008.

The Bus People: Unit 1, Lesson 4

Impact of Disabilities on Families

Book: *The Bus People* by Rachel Anderson. 1989. Grade 7+	
Global Purpose: To understand and accept individuals with various severe disabilities.	
Objective: Students will understand the dependent and independent roles of family members of individuals with disabilities.	
Materials: paper and markers	
Pre-Reading Activities	• Ask students to create a "Family Relationships" map. Have them write their name in the middle of the paper and draw a circle around it. Then ask them to write the names of family members all around their name. Have them draw arrows between names to demonstrate members whom they specifically help and those who specifically help them. • Have students share their family maps in small groups focusing on the ways they help each other.
During Reading Activities	• Ask students to read Chapters 3 and 6 independently. • As they read, ask them to write down words that describe the relationship between Micky and his mother and between Thoby and his sister.
Post-Reading Activities	• Place students in small groups. Ask them to discuss their notes. • As a whole class, discuss the words they used to describe the relationship between Micky and his mother, Thoby and his sister. • Ask a parent and/or a sibling of a person with a severe disability to talk about their reciprocal relationship with that person (e.g., "How do you help him or her?" "How does he or she help you?") • As a class, read Chapter 8. • Discuss the ways in which this was both a typical day and an unusual day for Bertram.
Closure	• Ask students to draw a Family Relationship map for Micky and/or Thoby. • As a class, discuss how the relationship in their families are the same or different for their own family.

Freak the Mighty: Unit 2, Lesson 1

Dispelling Stereotypes: The Unvanquished Truth

Book: *Freak the Mighty* by Rodman Philbrick. 1993. Grade 7+

Global Purpose: To promote positive student attitudes toward persons with disabilities by focusing on their strengths.

Objective: Students will define *stereotype* and identify the negative effects of stereotypes, in general and in the book *Freak the Mighty.*

Materials: Internet access, *Don't Scan Me* video (http://www.freevibe.com/share/realteens/ads.asp), "Attitudes Toward Individuals with Disabilities" worksheet, student journals

Pre-Reading Activities	• Ask students to define *stereotype.* • Show the antidrug video titled *Don't Scan Me.* • Discuss how the video ties into the topic of stereotyping. • Ask students to think about a time when someone unfairly labeled them and to record in their journal how they felt.
During Reading Activities	• Ask the students to look for ways in which Kevin and Max are stereotyped in the book.
Post-Reading Activities	• Divide the class into six groups. Assign each group to review Chapters 1, 2, or 6 and to locate any adjectives used to label Kevin or Max (or both). • Ask each group to share what they found from their assigned chapter. Review specific examples together as a class. • In their groups have students complete the "Attitudes" worksheet while discussing the attitudes of various characters in the book toward Freak and Max.
Closure	• Tell the class that people with disabilities often face stereotypes because they at first appear to be so different from others. This unit focuses on understanding and accepting people with disabilities by focusing on their strengths and the similarities they share with the general population.

Attitudes Toward Individuals with Disabilities

Directions: Using this table, record the attitudes held by the various characters toward Max and Kevin. Be prepared to discuss whether the character's attitude changed during the story.

Character	Attitude Toward Max	Attitude Toward Kevin
Grim		
Gram		
Tony D.		
Gwen		
Max		
Kevin		
Iggy		
Loretta		
Mr. Kane		

From *Teaching About Disabilities Through Children's Literature* by Mary Anne Prater and Tina Taylor Dyches. Westport, CT: Teacher Ideas Press. Copyright © 2008.

Freak the Mighty: Unit 2, Lesson 2

To the Max: Success in the Face of Learning Disabilities

Book: *Freak the Mighty* by Rodman Philbrick. 1993. Grade 7+	
Global Purpose: To promote positive student attitudes toward persons with disabilities by focusing on their strengths.	
Objective: Students will describe a learning disability and ways in which they can help peers who have difficulty with academic work.	
Materials: Internet access, "Learning Preferences Questionnaires"	
Pre-Reading Activities	• Ask students to complete one of the learning preference questionnaires found at: www.engr.ncsu.edu/learningstyles/ilsweb.html, http://agelesslearner.com/assess/learningstyle.html, www.chaminade.org/inspire/learnstl.htm, or the Learning Preferences Checklist in Unit 5, Lesson 3. • If using an Internet questionnaire, ask students to print their results. • Ask: "What do these individuals have in common: Tom Cruise, Franklin D. Roosevelt, Ludwig von Beethoven, Helen Keller, Whoopi Goldberg?" [Answer: They all had/have disabilities. Tom Cruise and Whoopi Goldberg have learning disabilities.] • Point out that even though they have disabilities, these people were or are able to be extremely successful.
During Reading Activities	• Explain that individuals with learning disabilities often have difficulty learning to read, spell, understand math, or do other tasks that involve language. They often learn well in other ways. • Emphasize that individuals with learning disabilities are not stupid, and they can be successful. • Discuss how Max was affected by his learning disability. • Ask: "What other problems, besides difficulty learning, did Max experience in and out of school because of his struggle to learn? Why was Max suddenly able to make such an improvement in school?" Look for specific examples in the book.
Post-Reading Activities	• Discuss how teachers can help students with learning disabilities be more successful in school. Discuss what they can do to help their peers be more successful in school.
Closure	• Review the results of the learning preferences questionnaire. • Discuss the variety of learning preferences that exist in the class. • Affirm the need to respect each others' differences and be accepting of all people.

Freak the Mighty: Unit 2, Lesson 3

Little Big Man: The Mighty Freak

Book: *Freak the Mighty* by Rodman Philbrick. 1993. Grade 7+	
Global Purpose: To promote positive student attitudes toward persons with disabilities by focusing on their strengths.	
Objective: Students will demonstrate acceptance by creating an advertisement promoting the strengths of a character with disabilities.	
Materials: Movie: *The Mighty*, "Kevin's Strengths" worksheet, art supplies (e.g., poster board, paper, markers, scissors, glue)	
Pre-Reading Activities	• Show a clip of one of Kevin and Max's quests from the film adaptation of the book, *The Mighty*. • Ask students if they would like to have a friend like Kevin.
During Reading Activities	• Divide the class into groups of four or five students. Using the "Kevin's Strengths" worksheet, ask each group to locate five instances in the story in which Kevin's strengths come in handy. • Share their examples as a whole class. • Ask the class: "What effect does Kevin have on other people? Why was he able to get so much out of life?" • Have the students look up *vanquish* at the back of the book in Kevin's dictionary. Ask: In all of his quests with Max, what "dragons" was he successful in conquering?
Post-Reading Activities	• In their groups, ask students to design a movie poster or comic strip depicting Kevin (Freak) as a superhero using the strengths they identified. • Ask students to brainstorm ideas and devise a catchy slogan so that others will want to know more about their superhero. • As a class review the comments made about Kevin by Tony D. in Chapter 6. In this chapter, Kevin stands up for himself. This can be referred to as *self-advocating*. Discuss that many people with disabilities cannot self-advocate at this level. • Ask: "How would you respond to Tony D. if Kevin were unable to respond himself?"
Closure	• Ask the class to share any other ideas or comments about Kevin and what they have learned from him. • Preview the next lesson in which students will present their posters to the class.

Kevin's Strengths

Directions: Skim the book and as a group locate five instances in which Kevin's strengths are helpful to the situation. Write a brief summary and the page numbers where you find these cases.

Page #	Brief Summary
	1.
	2.
	3.
	4.
	5.

From *Teaching About Disabilities Through Children's Literature* by Mary Anne Prater and Tina Taylor Dyches. Westport, CT: Teacher Ideas Press. Copyright © 2008.

Freak the Mighty: Unit 2, Lesson 4

Real Life Heroes: Our Peers with Disabilities

Book: *Freak the Mighty* by Rodman Philbrick. 1993. Grade 7+	
Global Purpose: To promote positive student attitudes toward persons with disabilities by focusing on their strengths.	
Objective: Students will express new, positive perspectives on the students with disabilities in their school.	
Materials: Prior arrangement with special education teacher, paper	
Pre-Reading Activities	• Complete the activities associated with Lesson 3
During Reading Activities	• Refer back to the excerpts from the book as needed.
Post-Reading Activities	• Ask each group to present its poster or comic strip to the class. Have group members tell which incidents in the book led to their characterization of Kevin. • Arrange for a special education teacher to speak to the class and profile a few special education students who are real-life heroes because they have struggled and overcome some obstacles in their lives. • If appropriate, invite the special education students to be present during this time. • After the special education teacher and students leave, ask students to write a one-page story about the quest of one of the visiting students to slay a personal dragon.
Closure	• When the stories are completed, combine them into separate books, one for each of the students profiled. • Deliver the stories to the respective students in their classroom.

I Am an Artichoke: Unit 3, Lesson 1

Defining Normal and Abnormal Behavior

Book: *I Am an Artichoke* by Lucy Frank. 1995. Grade 7+	
Global Purpose: To increase understanding of and friendships with individuals with emotional and behavioral disorders.	
Objective: Students will identify that context helps determine what is normal and abnormal.	
Materials: Worksheets "What Is Normal?" Parts 1 and 2, colored pencils	
Pre-Reading Activities	• Divide students into groups of three or four. Ask them to complete the "What is Normal?" Part 1 worksheet. • Ask each group to share its results and experiences with the class. • Discuss how what is normal is bound by context. • Ask the groups to create additional information for each scenario that makes each situation either normal or abnormal. • Have students share their contextual information with the whole class.
During Reading Activities	• While individually reading the book, ask students to identify two behaviors each for Emily, Sarah, and Florence (total = 6) to be discussed later (e.g., Emily constantly using the exercise bicycle).
Post-Reading Activities	• Place students in their same group of three or four students. Have them share their lists of behaviors. Using the "What Is Normal Part 2" worksheet, ask them to select one behavior for each character, create an opinion line similar to the pre-reading activity. Carry out the activity as the students did before reading the book. • Discuss whether the context helps them interpret a behavior as either normal or abnormal. • Share other examples of how context determines whether a behavior is normal or not. • Discuss how we need to be careful not to prejudge people by seeing their behavior out of context.
Closure	• Remind students that normal is based on context and the importance of not prejudging people.

What Is Normal?
Part 1

Directions: Ask a group to read each scenario. Then, based on your feelings, individually, but <u>simultaneously</u>, mark on the line indicating how normal or abnormal you believe the behavior is. (Hint: It may be helpful for each member to use a different colored pen or pencil.)

---

1. You have a new neighbor. One evening you notice that the parents deliberately lock their fifteen-year-old son out of the house. You are not certain when or if the boy is allowed back into the house. The parents' behavior is:

Normal   Abnormal

_____

---

2. A classmate invites you over to his house after school. While there, you hear him "mouthing off" to his mother. Although he doesn't use profanity, he talks back and tells her he's not going to do what she wants him to do in a rude fashion. The classmate's behavior is:

Normal   Abnormal

_____

---

3. You've noticed that your teenage sister is avoiding dinnertime more and more. When she does sit down at the table with your family, she plays with her food instead of eating it. Based on comments she's made and just observing her, you know she would rather be out running at the park or on her exercise bicycle. Your sister's behavior is:

Normal   Abnormal

_____

Select the scenario for which there is the most disagreement and discuss it. Try to reach consensus.

What Is Normal?
Part 2

Directions: Based on your individual lists of behaviors, as a group identify one behavior for each character. Describe it in writing under the person's name. Then, based on your feelings, individually, but <u>simultaneously</u>, mark on the line indicating how normal or abnormal you believe the behavior is. (Hint: It may be helpful for each member to use a different colored pen or pencil.)

---

1. Sarah's Behavior:

Normal   Abnormal

_____

---

2. Emily's Behavior:

Normal   Abnormal

_____

---

3. Florence's Behavior:

Normal   Abnormal

_____

Select the scenario where there is the most disagreement and discuss. Try to reach consensus.

I Am an Artichoke: Unit 3, Lesson 2

Understanding Persons with EBDs

Book: *I Am an Artichoke* by Lucy Frank. 1995. Grade 7+	
Global Purpose: To increase understanding of and friendships with individuals who have emotional or behavioral disorders (EBDs).	
Objective: To recognize the symptoms of and types of services available to individuals with EBDs.	
Materials: Emotional/Behavioral Disorders Quiz, Emotional/Behavioral Disorders Answer Key	
Pre- and During Reading Activities	• Students should have read the book prior to this lesson.
Post-Reading Activities	• Review the concept that normal is based on context. • Describe how there are certain disorders that are usually manifested by behavior and that professionals have classified them into categories. Note that you will be discussing some of these disorders in today's lesson. • Have students complete the EBD quiz individually. Place students in pairs and ask them to compare answers and discuss. Working with students as a full class, provide the answers with brief explanations. • Divide the class into six groups. Assign each group one of the following disorders: – Anxiety disorder (excluding obsessive-compulsive) – Obsessive-compulsive disorder – Severe depression – Bipolar disorder – Conduct disorder – Schizophrenia • Explain that you will discuss eating disorders in more detail in a later lesson. – Ask students to locate as much information as they can about the assigned disorder and typical services for those with each disorder in the twenty-minute block provided. Then provide ten minutes for them to prepare a presentation for the class on the symptoms and types of services available. – Student groups present to the class. – Discuss the difference between these disorders and individuals who may behave differently but not have an EBD. Generate some examples as a class.
Closure	• Ask students to write down three new things that they learned from this lesson. For each of the three, describe how they could apply this new information to help themselves, a friend, or a family member.

Emotional/Behavioral Disorders Quiz

True/False

1. Young people who experience excessive fear, worry, or uneasiness may have an anxiety disorder.

2. As many as 10 percent of all young people have an anxiety disorder.

3. Obsessive-compulsive disorders cause children to become "trapped" in patterns of repeated thoughts and behaviors, such as washing hands or repeatedly counting certain objects or actions.

4. Severe depression does not occur in childhood.

5. When individuals are depressed, their thoughts often change; for example, they may believe that they are ugly, unable to do anything right, or that their life is hopeless.

6. Exaggerated mood swings that range from extreme excitedness to depression is called bipolar disorder.

7. If a person shows little concern for others and repeatedly lies, steals, sets fires, is truant, or vandalizes, he or she may have a conduct disorder.

8. Eating disorders are rarely life threatening.

9. More females than males have eating disorders.

10. People with schizophrenia may experience hallucinations, delusions, and inability to experience pleasure.

From *Teaching About Disabilities Through Children's Literature* by Mary Anne Prater and Tina Taylor Dyches. Westport, CT: Teacher Ideas Press. Copyright © 2008.

Emotional/Behavioral Disorders Quiz
Answer Key

1. People who experience excessive fear, worry, or uneasiness may have an anxiety disorder. *TRUE. Anxiety disorders are one of the most common disorders found in childhood.*

2. About 10 percent of all young people have an anxiety disorder. *FALSE. Thirteen percent of all young people between the ages nine and seventeen may have an anxiety disorder.*

3. Obsessive-compulsive disorders cause children to become "trapped" in patterns of repeated thoughts and behaviors, such as washing hands or repeatedly counting certain objects or actions. *TRUE. Obsessive-compulsive disorder is considered a type of anxiety disorder.*

4. Severe depression does not occur in childhood. *FALSE. This was once believed to be true. Now experts agree that severe depression can occur at any age. In fact up to 2 percent of all children and 8 percent of all adolescents may be severely depressed.*

5. When individuals are depressed, their thoughts often change; for example, they may believe that they are ugly, unable to do anything right, or that their life is hopeless. *TRUE. Depression may be seen by changes in emotions, motivation, physical well-being, and thoughts.*

6. Exaggerated mood swings that range from extreme excitedness to depression is called bipolar disorder. *TRUE. This disorder was previously called manic depression.*

7. If a person shows little concern for others and repeatedly lies, steals, sets fires, is truant, or vandalizes, he or she may have a conduct disorder. *TRUE. Individuals with conduct disorder commit offenses that often grow more serious over time. Current estimates are that 1 to 4 percent of nine to seventeen year olds have a conduct disorder.*

8. Eating disorders are rarely life-threatening. *FALSE. Eating disorders can be very life-threatening.*

9. More females than males have eating disorders. *TRUE. Anorexia affects between .5 to 1 percent of all adolescent girls, with a much smaller number of boys being affected.*

10. People with schizophrenia may experience hallucinations, delusions, and inability to experience pleasure. *TRUE. They may also experience withdrawal from others and loss of contact with reality.*

Source: The U.S. Department of Health and Human Services, National Mental Health Information Center:
http://mentalhealth.samhsa.gov/child.

I Am an Artichoke: Unit 3, Lesson 3

Understanding Eating Disorders

Book: *I Am an Artichoke* by Lucy Frank. 1995. Grade 7+	
Global Purpose: To increase understanding of and friendships with individuals who have emotional or behavioral disorders.	
Objective: Students will identify the symptoms of eating disorders and the ways to access help.	
Materials: Internet access, PBS video (*Eating Disorders on America's College Campuses*; http://www.pbs.org/merrow/rss/media/60.mp4; transcript: http://www.pbs. org/merrow/podcast/transcripts/60_EatingDisorders.pdf), and *KID* video (http://www. nedic.ca/videos/psa.shtml)	
Pre-Reading Activities	• As a class discuss what the students know about eating disorders, their symptoms, and the forms of help that are available. • Describe that students will be reading a book about a girl with anorexia.
During Reading Activities	• While reading, ask students to look for specific examples or events that happen in the story that indicate Emily has an eating disorder.

Post-Reading Activities	• Watch the PBS video, *Eating Disorders on America's College Campuses*
	• Ask students to listen for answers to these questions:
	  – How much exercising is considered compulsive?
	  – What are some consequences of purging?
	  – What are two potential causes of eating disorders?
	  – What is "tray gazing?"
	  – How are control and eating disorders related?
	  – Why do eating disorders have little to do with food?
	  – What percent of women on college campuses have an eating disorder?
	  – What traits are associated with eating disorders?
	• Discuss the answers to these questions as a class.
	• Ask what characteristics the students saw in Emily that are similar to what they learned from the video.
	• Watch the video labeled *KID*
	• Ask students:
	  – How would you feel if others called you these names?
	  – How would you feel if you called yourself these names?
	  – How could you help a friend who did this to herself?
	• Generate specific ways to help friends in this situation.

Closure	• Assign groups to identify resources available in the school and community to help those with eating disorders and then report back to the class.

I Am an Artichoke: Unit 3, Lesson 4

Developing Friendships: What Should I Say?

Book: *I Am an Artichoke* by Lucy Frank. 1995. Grade 7+	
Global Purpose: To increase understanding of and friendships with individuals who have emotional or behavioral disorders.	
Objective: To understand how students can show friendship to those who have EBDs.	
Materials: "Talking with Individuals with EBDs" worksheet, personal journals	
Pre- and During Reading Activities	• Students should have read the book prior to this lesson.
Post-Reading Activities	• Review previous lessons. • Teach the tips for talking to a friend who may have EBD (see "Talking with Individuals with EBDs" worksheet). • In pairs or small groups, ask students to complete the "Talking with Individuals with EBDs" worksheet to identify examples of how Sarah demonstrated these tips with Emily. Report back to the whole class. • Ask students to think of someone they know who might have an EBD. Remind them to keep the names and relationships (e.g., my sister) private. • Ask them to write in their journals how any of these tips have helped them in the past or will help them in the future. If they don't know someone, they can use Sarah and Emily as examples, elaborating on what Emily did well and how she could improve in her interactions with Sarah.
Closure	• Review the tips with students and challenge them to find ways to use these tips when interacting with family and friends.

Talking with Individuals with EBDs

Directions: Identify one example in the book for each of these tips. Write that example below.

Tip	Page Number(s)	Description of Interaction Between Sarah and Emily
Find time to talk.		
Share your concerns.		
Ask her to seek help.		
Avoid conflicts with the person.		
Don't place blame, shame, or guilt on the person.		
Avoid giving simple solutions.		
Express your continued support.		

Source: National Eating Disorders Association: http://www.nedic.ca.

From *Teaching About Disabilities Through Children's Literature* by Mary Anne Prater and Tina Taylor Dyches. Westport, CT: Teacher Ideas Press. Copyright © 2008.

Joey Pigza Loses Control: Unit 4, Lesson 1

Characteristics of Attention-Deficit/Hyperactive Disorder (ADHD)

Book: *Joey Pigza Loses Control* by Jack Gantos. 2000. Grade 7+	
Global Purpose: To increase students' awareness and understanding of persons with ADHD.	
Objective: Students will identify general characteristics of ADHD.	
Materials: "Simulation Activities" sheet, "Quick Facts About ADHD" sheet	
Pre-Reading Activities	• Conduct Activities 1 and 2 as described on the *Simulation Activities* sheet. • Ask students what they know about ADHD. • Discuss the definition and characteristics of ADHD (see "Quick Facts About ADHD").
During Reading Activities	• While they are reading the book individually, ask students to identify reading passages that identify ADHD symptoms in Joey.
Post-Reading Activities	• Discuss as a class the characteristics of ADHD that they found in the reading passages about Joey. Identify which of the bulleted characteristics on the Quick Facts sheet they found in the book.
Closure	• Review the characteristics of ADHD. Emphasize that not all individuals with ADHD have the same characteristics and that only well-qualified professionals can diagnose ADHD.

Simulation Activities

Activity 1—Following Directions

Tell students that you are going to give them a list of things to do that they must do in order. Tell them to wait until all of the directions are given before they start. Then provide a list of ten unrelated directions, such as:

- Stomp your foot two times.
- Shake hands with someone.
- Place your math book on top of your desk.
- Stand up and walk around your desk.
- Sit down.
- Write your name on a piece of paper.
- Take off your right shoe.
- Clap your hands three times.
- Put away all materials on your desk.
- Put your head down on your desk.

Discuss how difficult it was to do all ten directions and in order mostly because there were more directions than they could remember at one time. Explain that students with attention problems sometimes feel this way even when simple directions are given.

Activity 2—Paying Attention

Provide students with a short reading passage, preferably from one of their textbooks. Disseminate only one of the following written directions to each student.

Read the paragraph assigned. Count how many letter s's there are in the passage. You have two minutes.

Read the paragraph assigned. Identify all of the verbs. You have two minutes.

Read the paragraph assigned. Identify (ask students to identify information related to the content they are reading). You have two minutes.

Provide students two minutes to follow their directions. Then remove all of the reading passages and directions from their desks and ask the students to answer these three questions:

1. How many s's are in the passage?
2. What verbs were used?
3. What was this reading passage about?

Discuss students' frustration with not knowing the answers they were assigned. Explain that some students have difficulty with schoolwork because they pay attention to the wrong things (e.g., counting s's) and therefore miss important information (e.g., reading comprehension).

Quick Facts About ADHD

- Attention-deficit/hyperactivity disorder (ADHD) is a condition found in some children. It is hard for these individuals to control their behavior, pay attention, or both. Because most children have difficulty in these areas, it is important that a thorough examination be conducted by a well-qualified professional before ADHD is diagnosed.

- Between 3 and 5 percent of children have ADHD, or approximately 2 million children in the United States.

- The major characteristics of ADHD are **inattention, hyperactivity,** and **impulsivity.** Children with ADHD may be daydreamers, have difficulty sitting still, or act before thinking.

- Different symptoms may appear in different settings, depending on the demands of the situation. Children with ADHD may have difficulty paying attention at school but don't have the same problem at home.

- ADHD is not easy to diagnose. Trained professionals must make the diagnosis.

- Below are some typical characteristics of ADHD. Individuals with ADHD will not necessarily exhibit all of these symptoms:

  - Feeling restless, often fidgeting with hands or feet, or squirming while seated
  - Running, climbing, or leaving a seat in situations when sitting or quiet behavior is expected
  - Blurting out answers before hearing the whole question
  - Having difficulty waiting in line or taking turns
  - Often becoming easily distracted by irrelevant sights and sounds
  - Often failing to pay attention to details and making careless mistakes
  - Rarely following instructions carefully and completely
  - Losing or forgetting things needed for a task
  - Often skipping from one uncompleted activity to another
  - Often has trouble sustaining attention during tasks or play
  - Seeming not to listen even when spoken to directly
  - Has difficulty following through on instructions
  - Often forgets
  - Talks excessively
  - Often interrupts or intrudes on others' conversations or games

Sources: National Institute of Mental Health: www.nimh.nih.gov/publicat/adhd.cfm; Mayo Clinic: www.mayoclinic.com/health/adhd/DS00275/DSECTION=2.

Joey Pigza Loses Control: Unit 4, Lesson 2

Attitudes Toward Disabilities

Book: *Joey Pigza Loses Control* by Jack Gantos. 2000. Grade 7+	
Global Purpose: To increase students' awareness and understanding of persons with ADHD.	
Objective: Students will identify how different individuals treated Joey and how they treat other individuals.	
Materials: "Attitudes" worksheet, student journals	
Pre-Reading Activities	• Explain that sometimes different individuals treat the same person in different ways. Ask students to identify a situation in which they are treated differently by two different persons. • Discuss how individuals with disabilities are also treated differently by different people.
During Reading Activities	• Ask students to brainstorm ideas of how Joey was treated differently by different people. Ask students to locate a few passages in the book.
Post-Reading Activities	• Place students in pairs. Ask them to fill out the "Attitudes" worksheet. • Lead a brief discussion with the class on how the attitudes of various characters affect the way they treat Joey and how they affect Joey himself. • Break the class into four groups. Assign each group one of the following characters: Joey's mother, Joey's father, Joey's Grandma, Leezy. Have students create a skit portraying the manner in which each interacted with Joey. Then, if necessary, ask them to portray a more positive relationship. • Discuss how the students can use the information they have learned in developing relationships with others, particularly those with disabilities.
Closure	• Ask students to identify one person whom they think they could treat better than they currently do and to describe in their journals specifically how they will treat this person better. • Challenge students to implement the ideas they generated in their journal.

Attitudes Worksheet

Directions: Based on your reading, locate a passage that demonstrates how each character acts toward Joey and how he acts toward them. Write a brief summary in each box. Include the page numbers where each was located.

Character	Attitude Toward Joey	Joey's Attitude Toward Him or Her
Joey's Mother		
Joey's Father		
Joey's Grandmother		
Leezy		
Other Characters		

Joey Pigza Loses Control: Unit 4, Lesson 3

Treatment of ADHD

Book: *Joey Pigza Loses Control* by Jack Gantos. 2000. Grade 7+	
Global Purpose: To increase students' awareness and understanding of persons with ADHD.	
Objective: Students will identify treatments found to be effective for individuals with ADHD.	
Materials: ADHD Treatment Quiz, ADHD Treatment Quiz Answer Key, reference materials (books, Internet)	
Pre-Reading Activities	• Have students complete the ADHD Treatment Quiz • Discuss the answers as a class.
During Reading Activities	• Place students in pairs. Ask them to locate specific passages in the book that discuss how Joey's ADHD was treated. • Ask: "How was Joey's treatment different or the same from what we just discussed?"

Post-Reading Activities	• Place students into groups of four.
	• Ask each group to research one or more of the following questions:
	  – What does the Food and Drug Administration say about the patch as treatment for ADHD?
	  – For whom is the patch recommended, and where is it worn?
	  – How long does the medication in a patch usually last?
	  – How expensive are the patches?
	  – About how many children are using patches today compared with those who use oral medication?

Closure	• Have students present the answers to the questions. • Discuss why they think Joey used a patch instead of oral medication and whether it was a good choice for him.

ADHD Treatment Quiz

True/False

1. Stimulant drugs are the most commonly prescribed medications for treating ADHD in children and adults.

2. Children with ADHD respond well to behavior management techniques, such as token reward systems and timeouts.

3. Children with ADHD rarely need social skills training because they already exhibit appropriate social behaviors.

4. The only medications that work for those with ADHD are stimulants.

5. Behavior management and medications are the most thoroughly researched treatments for ADHD.

6. Biofeedback has been proved to help those with ADHD change their brainwave patterns to more normal ones.

7. Studies have linked diet to improved ADHD characteristics. Specifically, diets that eliminate additives, as well as foods such as sugar, caffeine, wheat, milk, and eggs, improve behavior in those with ADHD.

8. The most common side effects of stimulants in children are decreased appetite, corresponding weight loss, nervousness, and problems sleeping.

9. Dietary supplements, such as fatty acids, ginkgo, or megadoses of vitamins, can reduce ADHD symptoms.

10. If a child is overmedicated (i.e., the dose is too high), he or she may develop jerky muscle movements, such as grimaces or twitches.

11. The best treatment for most children is a combined behavior management and medication approach.

12. Dependence on stimulant medication has been reported in children who take medications orally and at the proper dosage.

ADHD Treatment Quiz
Answer Key

True/False

1. Stimulant drugs are the most commonly prescribed medications for treating ADHD in children and adults. *TRUE. The most commonly used stimulants include Ritalin, Concerta, Adderall, and Dexedrine.*

2. Children with ADHD respond well to behavior management techniques, such as token reward systems and timeouts. *TRUE. Behavior management techniques have proved especially beneficial for people with ADHD.*

3. Children with ADHD rarely need social skills training because they already exhibit appropriate social behaviors. *FALSE. Social skills training can help children learn appropriate social behaviors that they may be lacking.*

4. The only medications that work for those with ADHD are stimulants. *FALSE. Another medication that works is not a stimulant and is atomoxetine (Strattera). Sometimes antidepressants are also used, especially in adults and in children who don't respond to the other medications.*

5. Behavior management and medications are the most thoroughly researched treatments for ADHD. *TRUE.*

6. Biofeedback has been proved to help those with ADHD change their brainwave patterns to more normal ones. *FALSE. This approach is being studied but is still considered unproved and experimental.*

7. Studies have linked diet to improved ADHD characteristics. Specifically, diets that eliminate additives, as well as foods such as sugar, caffeine, wheat, milk, and eggs, improve behavior in those with ADHD. *FALSE. Although a great deal of media attention has focused on diets for ADHD, no consistent links have been found between diet and improved symptoms of ADHD.*

8. The most common side effects of stimulants in children are decreased appetite, corresponding weight loss, nervousness, and problems sleeping. *TRUE. These are the most common side effects. Adjustments in dosage can often offset these side effects.*

9. Dietary supplements, such as fatty acids, ginkgo, or megadoses of vitamins, can reduce ADHD symptoms. *FALSE. There is no evidence that these supplements can reduce ADHD symptoms.*

10. If a child is overmedicated (i.e., the dose is too high), he or she may develop jerky muscle movements, such as grimaces or twitches. *TRUE. A small percentage of children may develop these symptoms, but they usually disappear when the medication dose is lowered.*

11. The best treatment for most children is a combined behavior management and medication approach. *TRUE. Research shows that using both a behavior management program and medication is the most effective treatment for most children with ADHD.*

12. Dependence on stimulant medication has been reported in children who take medications orally and at the proper dosage. *FALSE. Dependence has not been reported because drug levels in the brain rise too slowly to produce a "high."*

Source: Mayo Clinic: www.mayoclinic.com/health/adhd/DS00275/DSECTION=7.

Joey Pigza Loses Control: Unit 4, Lesson 4

Read All About It!

Book: *Joey Pigza Loses Control* by Jack Gantos. 2000. Grade 7+	
Global Purpose: To increase students' awareness and understanding of persons with ADHD.	
Objective: Students will create a newspaper article on ADHD including information they've learned about ADHD, using Joey as the example in their article.	
Materials: Reference materials, previous handouts	
Pre-Reading Activities	• Students should have read this book prior to this lesson.
During Reading Activities	• Tell students that they will be writing a newspaper article on ADHD as a small group. The article will include Joey as the example in their article. Provide the following list of items to be included: – Typical characteristics of ADHD – Prevalence rates – Research-based treatments for ADHD – One or two illustrations or photographs – Descriptions or quotations from Joey interspersed as their example • Encourage students to find specific quotations and examples from the book as they are writing their articles.
Post-Reading Activities	• Create a booklet with each article included. Make copies for all of the students.
Closure	• Remind students that many aspects about ADHD remain known. Encourage students to pay attention when they hear or read news reports about ADHD to keep their own knowledge base up-to-date.

Tru Confessions: Unit 5, Lesson 1

Etiology of Disabilities: The Mutant Shark Person

Book: *Tru Confessions* by Janet Tashjian. 1997. Grade 7+	
Global Purpose: To recognize positive contributions of those who are different from us.	
Objective: Students will recognize and dispel false beliefs about how some disabilities are caused.	
Materials: "Causes of Disabilities" worksheet, Internet access	
Pre-Reading Activities	• Students should read the entire book before beginning this unit. • Ask students if they have ever known people who thought they could "catch" a disability by touching or otherwise interacting with a person who has a disability. Discuss the differences between communicable diseases and intellectual or physical disabilities. • Ask the students if they know what *etiology* means. Discuss etiologies of a few conditions, such as Down syndrome, Fragile X syndrome, and Williams syndrome.
During Reading Activities	• Review pages 9, 57, 81, and 98, where Tru writes about how Eddie became disabled because of asphyxia when he was born. • Why did Tru think that she was a "mutant shark person who thrashed and fought in the womb, trying to kill my twin, but instead just ended up handicapping him" (p. 81)?
Post-Reading Activities	• Have students complete the "Causes of Disabilities" worksheet, allowing them thirty to forty minutes to do so. Then have them report the answers they found and discuss the similarities and differences found on various Web sites. • Explain that we currently do not know the etiologies of most disabilities. However, we do know how to reduce the occurrence of some of them (e.g., not drinking or smoking while pregnant, consuming sufficient folic acid while pregnant). • Discuss how to determine whether the information from these Web sites is trustworthy or not (e.g., Web sites that base their information on current research, those that report similar information that does not go contrary to common knowledge or current research). • Discuss any reported etiologies from the Web sites that do not appear to be based on sound research.
Closure	• Discuss how Tru was Eddie's strongest supporter and not a "mutant shark person" who caused him to have a disability.

Causes of Disabilities

Directions: Conduct an Internet search to find reported causes of the disabilities listed below. Find information from at least three sites, and record this information in the table. Provide the URL for each Web site.

Disability	Website #1 URL:	Website #2 URL:	Website #3 URL:
Autism			
Blindness			
Deafness			
Dyslexia			
Learning Disabilities			
Mental Retardation			
Stuttering			

From *Teaching About Disabilities Through Children's Literature* by Mary Anne Prater and Tina Taylor Dyches. Westport, CT: Teacher Ideas Press. Copyright © 2008.

Tru Confessions: Unit 5, Lesson 2

Avoiding Victimization: "I Don't Want to Be Different"

Book: *Tru Confessions* by Janet Tashjian. 1997. Grade 7+	
Global Purpose: To recognize positive contributions of those who are different from us.	
Objective: Students will demonstrate understanding of how to avoid and prevent bullying by engaging in role-plays.	
Materials: *Tru Confessions* Disney Original Movie (2002), "Protector, Not Perpetrator" pledge sheet	
Pre-Reading Activities	• Show the video clip from the Disney Original Movie depicting the scene in which Billy Meier and his friends bully Eddie and Tru (pp. 89–95).
During Reading Activities	• Review pages 109–113 where Eddie becomes claustrophobic in the mall.
	• Why do you think Eddie told Tru, "I don't want to be different. I want to be the same. Same as everybody else"? Are there any other times when Eddie has this acute sense of self-awareness? Does Eddie generally seem to be happy or upset with the way he is?
	• Review pages 89–95 where Billy Meier and his friends take advantage of Eddie because of his special needs. Have you ever witnessed anyone teasing or bullying someone who is "different"? How did the person being bullied react?
Post-Reading Activities	• Divide the students into small groups where they role-play one situation in two different ways: first, a case in which the victim is unable to defend himself or herself and therefore needs a protector or advocate and second, a case in which the victim defends himself or herself from the bully. Caution the students to be sensitive when depicting those who are vulnerable (e.g., do not make fun of or stereotype them).
Closure	• Discuss how individuals with disabilities are often victimized because they honestly trust others, they want to gain acceptance, or they don't have the skills to defend themselves.
	• Have the students sign the "Protector, Not Perpetrator" pledge never to bully, taunt, or victimize vulnerable individuals.

Protector, Not Perpetrator

I, _____ pledge that I will not bully, tease, taunt, or otherwise victimize vulnerable people. Further, when I see perpetrators victimizing others, I will do all in my power to protect the victims.

Those who are vulnerable include people such as:

- People younger than I am

- People weaker than I am

- People not as confident or smart as I am

- People with disabilities

- Anyone I feel that I could dominate or coerce

Signed this _____ day of _____ , _____.
            (day)   (month)   (year)

Protector's Signature:

_____

Witness' Signature:

_____

From *Teaching About Disabilities Through Children's Literature* by Mary Anne Prater and Tina Taylor Dyches. Westport, CT: Teacher Ideas Press. Copyright © 2008.

Tru Confessions: Unit 5, Lesson 3

Accepting Differences: Just Who Has Special Needs?

Book: *Tru Confessions* by Janet Tashjian. 1997. Grade 7+	
Global Purpose: To recognize positive contributions of those who are different from us.	
Objective: Students will recognize strengths and challenges in all people without focusing on weaknesses.	
Materials: "Learning Preferences Checklist," "Eddie's Strengths and Challenges" worksheet, and "My Strengths and Challenges" worksheet	
Pre-Reading Activities	• Give students the "Learning Preferences Checklist" to complete. Have them discuss their individual preferences with a partner. Then determine whether anyone in the class has exactly the same learning preferences. Note that all students have special preferences and needs to learn effectively.
During Reading Activities	• Review page 21 where Tru describes Eddie's special needs. • Review page 14, where Tru describes her special needs, and pages 19–20, where she describes her mother's special needs. • Have students individually complete "Eddie's Strengths and Challenges."
Post-Reading Activities	• Have the students individually complete "My Strengths and Challenges" worksheet. Have the students share their strengths and challenges with a partner.
Closure	• Remind the students that we all have special needs because we are all different from each other. Our individual strengths and challenges differ. When we focus on our strengths, our challenges do not become hardships.

Learning Preferences Checklist

I like to learn in an environment that is:

Sound

_____ quiet

_____ somewhat quiet

_____ noisy

Light

_____ brightly lit

_____ dimly lit

_____ dark

Temperature

_____ warm

_____ cool

Design

_____ formal

_____ informal

_____ organized

_____ somewhat organized

When I learn, I like to:

Social

_____ work alone

_____ work with one peer or a small group

_____ work with a teacher

_____ work with a teacher and group of peers

When I learn, I like to:

Movement

_____ sit still until I finish

_____ get up and then return to work

_____ move about a great deal

When I learn, I:

Intake

_____ eat/drink something

_____ don't eat/drink something

_____ sometimes eat/drink something

In school I usually am:

Motivation

_____ self-motivated

_____ peer-motivated

_____ authority-motivated

_____ unmotivated

Persistence

_____ persistent (finish what I begin)

_____ fairly persistent

_____ not persistent

Responsibility

_____ responsible (do what I should do)

_____ fairly responsible

_____ not responsible

I tend to learn and remember:

Perception

_____ what I hear

_____ what I see

_____ what I feel, touch, or do

I work best with:

Structure

_____ clear directions, few choices, specific time limits

_____ few directions, many choices, flexible deadlines

My best learning time is:

Time of Day

_____ early morning

_____ late morning

_____ early afternoon

_____ late afternoon

_____ evening

Eddie's Strengths and Challenges

Directions: Look through *Tru Confessions* and identify three of Eddie's strengths and three of his challenges. Write these in the table below, including the page numbers where you found them.

Strengths	Page Number	Challenges	Page Number

From *Teaching About Disabilities Through Children's Literature* by Mary Anne Prater and Tina Taylor Dyches. Westport, CT: Teacher Ideas Press. Copyright © 2008.

My Strengths and Challenges

Directions: In the table below, write at least one of your strengths and one of your challenges for each area.

Social	Intellectual/Academic
Physical	**Emotional/Spiritual**

Tru Confessions: Unit 5, Lesson 4

Growing Up: Spinning into Separate Futures

Book: *Tru Confessions* by Janet Tashjian. 1997. Grade 7+	
Global Purpose: To recognize positive contributions of those who are different from us.	
Objective: Students will demonstrate understanding of the importance of preparing students with disabilities for post-secondary experiences.	
Materials: "Future Planning Chart, "Eddie's Future Planning Chart"	
Pre-Reading Activities	• Give students the "Future Planning Chart" to complete. Have them discuss their goals for their future with a partner. Then discuss the types of support they will need to achieve their goals. • Inform the class that some students with disabilities are unable to participate in post-secondary activities because they don't have the services and supports necessary for them to be successful.
During Reading Activities	• Review page 147 where Tru realizes that she is not going to cure Eddie. How does Tru feel about her inability to cure him? • Does Eddie need to be cured? Why or why not? • Review pages 157–161 where Tru, Eddie, and their mother go to the theme park. Eddie likes to ride around in circles on the merry-go-round and on the duck ride. How does this analogy of "spinning into separate futures" relate to Eddie's future and Tru's future?
Post-Reading Activities	• Have the students complete "Eddie's Future Planning Chart" in pairs or small groups. Have the students share their plan with the whole class.
Closure	• Remind the class that it is important to include students with disabilities into normal daily activities as much as possible so that they can gain functional skills before they complete their high school education. Have them discuss ways they can include students with disabilities in their school and extracurricular activities.

Future Planning Chart

Directions: Write your desired outcome for each "Future Activity" based on your personal goals for when you complete high school. Then write at least two steps you must complete to achieve each desired outcome.

Future Activity	Desired Outcome *What do you want to achieve?*	Action Plan *What steps are necessary for you to be successful?*
Education University Community college Adult education classes Technical school Online courses Vocational training Community-based adult day programs		
Employment Competitive employment Supported job placement Full-time work Part-time work		
Community Experiences Housing Recreation Social relationships Transportation Independent living		
Daily Living Skills and Needs Income/benefits Insurance Cooking/cleaning Self-care		

From *Teaching About Disabilities Through Children's Literature* by Mary Anne Prater and Tina Taylor Dyches. Westport, CT: Teacher Ideas Press. Copyright © 2008.

Eddie's Future Planning Chart

Directions: Write your idea of a desired outcome for each of Eddie's "Future Activities" upon completion of high school. Then write at least two steps that must be completed in order to achieve each desired outcome.

Future Activity	Desired Outcome *What do you think Eddie wants to achieve?*	Action Plan *What steps are necessary for Eddie to be successful?*
Education University Community college Adult education classes Technical school Online courses Vocational training Community-based adult day programs		
Employment Competitive employment Supported job placement Full-time work Part-time work		
Community Experiences Housing Recreation Social relationships Transportation Independent living		
Daily Living Skills and Needs Income/benefits Insurance Cooking/cleaning Self-Care		

From *Teaching About Disabilities Through Children's Literature* by Mary Anne Prater and Tina Taylor Dyches. Westport, CT: Teacher Ideas Press. Copyright © 2008.

V. Activities and Reproducible Worksheets

Activity 1: Same and Different #1

Activity 2: Same and Different #2

Activity 3: Sibling's Reaction

Activity 4: Feelings

Activity 5: Write an Author

Activity 6: Reflection Journal

Activity 7: Attitudes

Activity 8: Roller-Movie

Activity 9: Retelling in a Different Time Period

Activity 10: Mock Children's Literature Award

Activity 11: Book Review

Activity 12: Write a Letter to a Character with Disabilities

Same and Different #1

Book: _____

Directions: After reading the book, complete the following table, comparing and contrasting at least five characteristics of yourself with the character with a disability.

This Is How We're Alike!

Character's Name:	My Name:
1.	1.
2.	2.
3.	3.
4.	4.
5.	5.

This Is How We're Different!

Character's Name: _____ **My Name:** _____

1.	1.
2.	2.
3.	3.
4.	4.
5.	5.

From *Teaching About Disabilities Through Children's Literature* by Mary Anne Prater and Tina Taylor Dyches. Westport, CT: Teacher Ideas Press. Copyright © 2008.

Same and Different #2

Directions: After reading the two books, complete the table comparing and contrasting the characters with similar disabilities.

Book: _____ Book: _____

Character's Name: _____ Character's Name: _____

This Is How They're Alike!

1.	1.
2.	2.
3.	3.
4.	4.
5.	5.

This Is How They're Different!

1.	**1.**
2.	**2.**
3.	**3.**
4.	**4.**
5.	**5.**

Sibling's Reaction

Directions: Write down how the sibling reacts to the behavior of the character with a disability. Then write down what you would *do* or how you might *feel* if you were in that sibling's situation.

Behavior of the Character with a Disability	Sibling's Reaction	My Reaction Would Be ...

Does the sibling change his or her feelings toward the behavior of the character with a disability? Give an example.

_____

_____

_____

From *Teaching About Disabilities Through Children's Literature* by Mary Anne Prater and Tina Taylor Dyches. Westport, CT: Teacher Ideas Press. Copyright © 2008.

Feelings

Directions: List some key experiences and feelings of the character with a disability in the spaces below. Find pictures on the Internet that represent these experiences and feelings. Upload the pictures to your PowerPoint file. Be sure to include the source for your pictures (e.g., google.com) on a reference page (final slide). Share your PowerPoint presentation with the class.

Key Experiences of the Character with a Disability	Feelings Related to These Experiences

Write an Author

Directions: After reading a book including a character with a disability, write the author of the book asking why he or she included a character with a disability.

Find the publisher's address (most authors are contacted via their publishers) and a contact name.

Postal: _____

_____

E-mail: _____

Draft the letter, including

☐ Your name and return address

    ☐ Author's name/address

    ☐ Date

    ☐ Greeting

    ☐ Introductory paragraph (who you are)

    ☐ Request (why you are writing)

    ☐ Concluding paragraph (how the author can respond, thanks)

    ☐ Salutation

    ☐ Your name

☐ Have a peer critique your letter.

☐ Revise the letter based on your peer's feedback.

☐ Send the letter.

Reflection Journal

Directions: After you have read

    ☐ one chapter

    ☐ ____ pages

    ☐ for one day

    ☐ for one week

    ☐ the entire book

Write in your response journal about:

    ☐ whatever you want to write regarding your reactions to the book

    ☐ how you would feel if you were a particular character

    ☐ what you would do if you were in a similar situation (describe the situation)

    ☐ how you have learned to accept or understand a character better

After you have completed your reflection journal, submit it to:

    ☐ the teacher

    ☐ a student in this class who has not read this book

    ☐ a student in this class who has read this book

Within one week, request a reply from the reviewer of your reflection journal.

Attitudes

Directions:

Before you read this book, assess your attitudes toward persons with disabilities by answering the following questions (adapted from *Attitudes Toward Disabled Persons Scale*, Yuker, Block, & Campbell, 1960).

____ Yes
____ No
    Students who have special needs may sometimes be just as intelligent as nondisabled people.

____ Yes
____ No
    People who have special needs are usually easier to get along with than other people.

____ Yes
____ No
    Most people who have special needs feel sorry for themselves.

____ Yes
____ No
    There shouldn't be special classes for people who have special needs.

____ Yes
____ No
    It would be best for people who have special needs to live and work in special places.

____ Yes
____ No
    Most people who have special needs worry a lot.

____ Yes
____ No
    People who have special needs are as happy as nondisabled people.

____ Yes
____ No
    People who have special needs tend to keep to themselves much of the time.

____ Yes
____ No
    You have to be careful of what you say when you are with people who have special needs.

____ Yes
____ No
    People with special needs are often grouchy.

After reading this book, answer the questions again.

___Yes
___No
Students who have special needs may sometimes be just as intelligent as nondisabled people.

___Yes
___No
People who have special needs are usually easier to get along with than other people.

___Yes
___No
Most people who have special needs feel sorry for themselves.

___Yes
___No
There shouldn't be special classes for people who have special needs.

___Yes
___No
It would be best for people who have special needs to live and work in special places.

___Yes
___No
Most people who have special needs worry a lot.

___Yes
___No
People who have special needs are as happy as nondisabled people.

___Yes
___No
People who have special needs tend to keep to themselves much of the time.

___Yes
___No
You have to be careful of what you say when you are with people who have special needs.

___Yes
___No
People with special needs are often grouchy.

Compare your answers. How did your attitudes change or remain the same as a result of reading this book?

Changed	Remained the Same

Roller-Movie

Directions: Illustrate scenes from the story on a long piece of shelf paper. Attach each end of the paper to a dowel rod. Cut a TV screen out of a cardboard box and insert the dowel rod in the top/bottom of the TV set. Show the appropriate scene as you retell the story.

Scenes to Depict	How These Scenes Will Be Illustrated

Retelling in a Different Time Period

Directions: Suppose the story took place

- ☐ 10
- ☐ 25
- ☐ 50
- ☐ 100
- ☐ 200

years ago. Write a summary of how the characters, setting, theme, and plot may have differed from the author's depiction.

	Author's Depiction	Your Depiction
Characters		
Setting		
Theme		
Plot		

Mock Children's Literature Award

Directions: After reading several books including a child with a disability, evaluate each book. Tally the results among the class and prepare a mock ceremony to announce the winners. Students can work in the following groups:

☐ Research Group—locate and acquire books

☐ Evaluation Group—prepare evaluation survey, tabulate results

☐ Awards Group—design and develop award certificates

☐ Ceremony Group—develop procedures for award ceremony, conduct ceremony

Book Review

Directions: After reading the book, write a brief review including what you did and did not like about the book. Then read one published review. Obtain an informal review from a parent of a child with the same type of disability of the character in the book you read. Compare the three reviews.

Personal Review	Published Review	Parent's Review

Write a Letter to a Character with Disabilities

Directions: Read a picture book that includes a character with disabilities, then write a letter to this character. Follow the format below.

Date_____

Dear _____,

I like how you _____.

I would like to play _____ **with you.**

I would like to be friends with you because _____

_____.

Sincerely,

_____
Name

VI. Additional Resources

Attention-Deficit/Hyperactivity Disorder

Prater, M. A., Johnstun, M., & Munk, J. (2005). From *Spaceman* to *The ADDed Touch*: Using juvenile literature to teach about attention-deficit disorder. *TEACHING Exceptional Children Plus, 1*(4) Article 4. Available online: http://escholarship.bc.edu/education/tecplus/vol1/iss4/art4/

Developmental Disabilities (Including Autism, Developmental Delay, Intellectual Disabilities, and Multiple Disabilities)

Dyches, T. T., & Prater, M. A. (2005). Characterization of developmental disabilities in children's fiction. *Education and Training in Developmental Disabilities, 40*, 202–216.

Dyches, T. T., & Prater, M. A. (2000). *Developmental disability in children's literature: Issues and annotated bibliography.* Reston, VA: Council for Exceptional Children.

Dyches, T. T., Prater, M. A., & Cramer, S. (2001). Mental retardation and autism in children's books. *Education and Training in Mental Retardation and Developmental Disabilities, 36*, 230–243.

Prater, M. A. (1999). Characterization of mental retardation in children's and adolescent literature. *Education and Training in Mental Retardation and Developmental Disabilities, 34*, 418–431.

Deafness/Hard of Hearing

Turner, N. D., & Traxler, M. (1997). Children's literature for the primary inclusive classroom: Increasing understanding of children with hearing impairments. *American Annals of the Deaf, 142*, 350–355.

Learning Disabilities

Prater, M. A. (2003). Learning disabilities in children's and adolescent literature: How are characters portrayed? *Learning Disability Quarterly, 26*, 47–62.

Various Disabilities

American Library Association: http://www.ala.org/ala/awardsbucket/schneideraward/bibliography.htm

Blaska, J. K. (2003). *Using children's literature to learn about disabilities and illness* (2nd ed.). Troy, NY: Educator's International Press.

Dyches, T. T., Prater, M. A., & Jenson, J. (2006). Caldecott books and their portrayal of disabilities. *TEACHING Exceptional Children Plus, 2*(5) Article 2. Available online: http://escholarship. bc.edu/education/tecplus/vol2/iss5/art2/

Hulen, L., Hoffbauer, D., & Prenn, M. (1998). Children's literature dealing with disabilities: A bibliography for the inclusive classroom. *Journal of Children's Literature*, 24(1), 67–77.

National Dissemination Center for Children with Disabilities http://www.nichcy.org/pubs/ bibliog/bib5txt.htm

Prater, M. A. (2000). Using juvenile literature that portrays characters with disabilities in your classroom. *Intervention in School and Clinic, 35,* 167–176.

Title Index

A Corner of the Universe, 7
A.D.D. not B.A.D., 2
Adam's Alternative Sports Day, 6
ADDed Touch, The, 2
Al Capone Does My Shirts, 6
Alphabet War, The, 34

Be Good to Eddie Lee, 27
Because of Winn-Dixie, 27
Ben Has Something to Say: A Story About Stuttering, 12
Ben, King of the River, 27
Best Worst Brother, The, 28
Big Mama, 41
Bird Boy, 12
Blabber Mouth, 13
Bringing Nettie Back, 48
Bus People, The, 28
By the Shores of Silver Lake, 48

Chuck Close Up Close, 41
Crazy Lady, 29
Crow Boy, 8
Cruise Control, 41
Curious Incident of the Dog in the Night-Time, The, 8
Cut, 22

Dad and Me in the Morning, 19
Dad, Jackie, and Me, 19
Deaf Child Crossing, 19
Dicey's Song, 35
Disabilities, 42
Double-Digit Club, The, 49
Dustin's Big School Day, 29

Eddie Enough!, 2

Flimflam Man, The, 13
Flying Solo, 14
Freak the Mighty, 35
From Charlie's Point of View, 50

Gentle's Holler, 50
Getting Near to Baby, 14
Gold in the Hills, 15
Great Gilly Hopkins, The, 51

Hard Life of Seymour E. Newton,The, 36
Harry and Willy and Carrothead, 42
Harry Sue, 42
Heck Superhero, 22
Hickory Chair, The, 51
Hooway for Wodney Wat, 15
How Many Days Until Tomorrow?, 37

I Am an Artichoke, 23
I Got a "D" in Salami, 37
Ian's Walk, 9
I'm Somebody Too, 3
Inside Out, 23

Jackson Whole Wyoming, 9
Joey Pigza Loses Control, 3
Joey Pigza Swallowed the Key, 4

Keeping Up with Roo, 30
King of the Wind, 16
Kissing Doorknobs, 24
Knockin' on Wood, 43
Knots on a Counting Rope, 52

Life Magic, 38
Little Women Next Door, 16

Mama Zooms, 43
Mandy, 20
Mary Marony and the Snake, 16
Me and Rupert Goody, 30
Melanie, 52
Moses Goes to a Concert, 20
Moses Sees a Play, 20
My Brother Sammy, 10
My Louisiana Sky, 31
My Name Is ~~Brain~~ Brian, 38

Nathan's Wish: A Story About Cerebral Palsy, 43
Niagara Falls, or Does It?, 39
Nick's Mission, 21
Nick's Secret, 21
Not as Crazy as I Seem, 24

Pay Attention, Slosh!, 4
Phoebe's Best Best Friend, 5
Planet of Junior Brown, The, 25
Printer, The, 21
Private School, 44

Ray Charles, 52
Reaching Dustin, 25
Ruby Mae Has Something to Say, 17
Rules, 10
Russ and the Almost Perfect Day, 31

Sarah's Sleepover, 52
Seal Surfer, 44
See the Ocean, 53
Shiniest Rock of All, The, 17
Silent Spillbills, The, 18
Sing to the Stars, 53
Small Steps, 44
So B. It, 32
Sparks, 32

Stuck in Neutral, 45
Summer of the Swans, The, 33
Summer School! What Genius Thought That Up?, 39
Susan Laughs, 45

Taco's Anyone?, 11
Tending to Grace, 18
Thank You, Mr. Falker, 40
These Happy Golden Years, 53
Things Not Seen, 54
Trevor Trevor, 11
Tru Confessions, 33
Tulip Touch, The, 26

View from Saturday, The, 46

Waiting for Mr. Goose, 5
We'll Paint the Octopus Red, 34
Westing Game, The, 46
Wheel on the School, The, 47
When She Was Good, 26
Whittington, 40
Wintering Well, 47

Yolondo's Genius, 11

Zipper, the Kid with ADHD, 5

Author Index

Anderson, Rachel, 28
Archambault, John, 52
Armstrong, Alan, 40
Avi, 44

Barasch, Lynne, 43
Barrett, Mary Brigid, 53
Bauer, Marion Dane, 49
Beard, Darleen Bailey, 13
Betancourt, Jeanne, 38
Blatchford, Claire H., 21
Booth, Barbara D., 20
Byars, Betsy, 33

Carrick, Carol, 52
Carter, Alden R., 29
Caseley, Judith, 42
Choldenko, Gennifer, 6
Clark, Joan, 9
Clements, Andrew, 53
Condra, Estelle, 53
Conly, Jane Leslie, 29
Cooper, Melrose, 38
Couloumbis, Audrey, 14
Cowen-Fletcher, Jane, 43
Crunk, Tony, 41

DeJong, Meindert, 47
DiCamillo, Kate, 27

Edwards, Becky, 10
Ellis, Marvie, 11

Fenner, Carol, 11
Fine, Anne, 26
Fleming, Virginia, 27
Fletcher, Ralph, 14
Foreman, Michael, 44
Frank, Lucy, 23
Fraustino, Lisa Rowe, 51
Fusco, Kimberly Newton, 18

Gantos, Jack, 3, 4
Gehret, Jeanne, 3
Gifaldi, David, 27
Gleitzman, Morris, 13
Glenn, Sharlee, 30
Greenberg, Jan , 41
Grove, Vicki, 25

Haddon, Mark, 8
Hamilton, Virginia, 25
Harrar, George, 24
Henry, Marguerite, 16
Herold, Ann Bixby, 36
Hesser, Terry Spencer, 24
Hill, Elizabeth Starr, 12
Holt, Kimberly Willis, 31

Janover, Caroline, 5, 37
Jordan, Sandra, 41

Klass, Sheila Solomon, 16
Kline, Suzy, 16
Konigsburg, E. L., 46

Lakin, Patricia, 19
Lawlor, Laurie, 15
Lears, Laurie, 5, 9, 12, 43
Leavitt, Martine, 22
Lester, Helen, 15
Lord, Cynthia, 10

Madden, Kerry, 50
Martin, Ann M., 7
Martin, Bill, Jr., 52
Mathis, Sharon Bell, 52
Matlin, Marlee, 19
Mazer, Norma Fox, 26
McKormick, Patricia, 22
McNamee, Graham, 32
Millman, Isaac, 20

O'Connor, Barbara, 30
Oliver, Lin, 37, 39

Paterson, Katherine, 51
Patterson, Nancy Ruth, 17
Penn, Audrey, 2
Philbrick, Rodman, 35
Polacco, Patricia, 40

Raskin, Ellen, 46
Rickert, Janet Elizabeth, 31
Robb, Diane Burton, 34
Roberts, Barbara, 5
Rodriguez, Bobbie, 52

Sachar, Louis, 44
Scrimger, Richard, 50
Seidler, Tor, 18
Small, David, 17
Smith, Mark, 4
Stauffacher, Sue, 42
Stuve-Bodeen, Stephanie, 28, 34

Tashjian, Janet, 33
Trueman, Terry, 23, 41, 45
Twachtman-Cullen, Diane, 11

Uhlberg, Myron, 19, 21

Vision, Mutiya, 42
Voigt, Cynthia, 35

Wait, Lea, 47
Watson, Robyn, 2
Weeks, Sarah, 32
Welton, Jude, 6
Wilder, Laura Ingalls, 48, 53
Willis, Jeanne, 45
Wilson, Nancy Hope, 48
Winkler, Henry, 37, 39

Yashima, Taro, 8

Zimmett, Debbie, 2

Award-Winning Books

A Corner of the Universe (Newbery Honor Book), 7
Al Capone Does My Shirts (Newbery Honor Book), 6

Because of Winn-Dixie (Newbery Honor Book), 27
By the Shores of Silver Lake (Newbery Honor Book), 48

Crazy Lady (Newbery Honor Book), 29
Crow Boy (Caldecott Honor Book), 8
Curious Incident of the Dog in the Night-Time, The (Dolly Gray Award), 8

Dicey's Song (Newbery Honor Book), 35

Getting Near to Baby (Newbery Honor Book), 14
Great Gilly Hopkins, The (Newbery Honor Book), 51

Ian's Walk (Dolly Gray Award), 9

Joey Pigza Loses Control (Newbery Honor Book), 3

Keeping Up with Roo (Dolly Gray Award), 30
King of the Wind (Newbery Honor Book), 16

Me and Rupert Goody (Dolly Gray Award), 30
My Brother Sammy (Dolly Gray Award), 10

Planet of Junior Brown, The (Newbery Honor Book), 25

Rules (Newbery Honor Book), 10

So B. It (Dolly Gray Award), 32
Summer of the Swans (Newbery Honor Book), 33

These Happy Golden Years (Newbery Honor Book), 53
Tru Confessions (Dolly Gray Award), 33

View from Saturday, The (Newbery Honor Book), 46

Westing Game, The (Newbery Honor Book), 46
Wheel on the School, The (Newbery Honor Book), 47
Whittington (Newbery Honor Book), 40

Yolanda's Genius (Newbery Honor Book), 11

About the Authors

MARY ANNE PRATER is Professor and Chairperson, Department of Counseling Psychology and Special Education, School of Education, Brigham Young University. She has written widely in journals and has two books published on this and related topics.

TINA TAYLOR DYCHES is Associate Professor Department of Counseling Psychology and Special Education Brigham Young University. Dr. Taylor has also published widely on this topic.